Women
FROM THE
Red-Light
District

Who Were In
God's Plans of
Salvation

REVEREND ELEANOR D. MILLER

WOMEN FROM THE RED-LIGHT DISTRICT
WHO WERE IN GOD'S PLANS OF SALVATION

iUniverse books may be ordered through booksellers or by contacting:

iUniverse
1663 Liberty Drive
Bloomington, IN 47403
www.iuniverse.com
844-349-9409

ISBN: 978-1-6632-3743-9 (sc)
ISBN: 978-1-6632-3744-6 (e)

Print information available on the last page.

iUniverse rev. date: 03/18/2022

The Bible is clear that the source
of salvation is Jesus Christ alone, and this book
is not to infer that there is any other way.
God's Plan of Salvation was through His sending
Jesus into the world to be the propitiation for the sins
of the whole world. Those who acknowledge, accept,
and receive Christ into their lives receives salvation.
This book is written to explain how God used different
women, some with questionable backgrounds to
fulfill His plan of salvation. The lives of those women
when viewed collectively were a fulfillment of God's
plans that led to His ultimate plan of Salvation,
the birth our Lord and Savior Jesus Christ.

Ephesians 2:8-9 NIV
*For it is by grace you have been saved, through
faith-and this is not from yourselves, it is the gift
of God-not by works, so that no one can boast.*

To all those persons who feel as if they have no value
because of some mistakes that you have made over the years,
this book is written to show that you do.
It is my prayers through these written words,
you will be illuminated to the truth,
that God sees beyond your faults,
and He stands ready to help you fulfill
the purpose for which you were created.
It may have been said, and you may have thought
that for you there is no help, nor hope,
but God can do the impossible.
He can clean you up and allow you to fit into
His plan of salvation.

Contents

Publisher's Preface

Reminiscing on my life and the years that have slowly drifted by makes me conclude regrettably that there were many days wasted and many mistakes made.

If it were possible to go back and undo the past, change some of the wrong decisions made and undo some of the iniquitous things done over the years, I would gladly do so. Realizing that those years are in the past, stored memories and recollections that fill a place where they can be visited but not accessible to where they can be altered sometimes sadden me. Therefore, what has already transpired good or bad, is accepted, the good with delight and the bad chalked up to lessons learned.

Recently someone made a post on a social media outlet that said "if I could redo this thing called life...I would do so much better and I would be so much better." There is a certainty that all have thought that same way; we have all regretted some of the things done in the past, however, one cannot live in the past. But retrospectively if a person had knowledge in the past to what they know in the present their actions and reactions to certain things would have probably been different. Since there is no going back to recalculate the past one must move forward; they must press on and let the past be the past, mistakes, and all.

Saint Paul says it so eloquently in **Philippians 3:13;** he says

"Forgetting those things which are behind, and reaching forth unto those things which are before, I press on..."

What gives a person the tenacity and fortitude to press on knowing they have made mistakes. The answer is when one accepts the Lord, Jesus Christ as their Savior the blood he shed on Calvary's cross cleanses them from the guilt associated with past sins and mistakes and gives that person a "second Chance."

Second chances do not eliminate the past but allows persons to understand that where others may see you as no good, or you feel within yourself that you are no good because of your past, you still have worth.

Damaged does not mean broken without the possibility of ever being repaired, remolded, or reshaped. Being broken means that a person is fragmented no longer complete, they are disconnected; however, all is not lost because it is possible that mending can take place.

Second Chance is a word used when giving items that some may think are of no use or of no value, an opportunity to be cleaned up and used to serve the same purpose as something new.

Yes, to those who can afford to, it is so easy to discard old things without regret and buy new things to replace the old rather than take the time to give the old items a makeover.

This same analogy of giving items a second chance, can also be applied to people; because there are people who need the opportunity to be refurbished; they need to be cleaned up and brought back to the brilliance that once existed in them when life was full of joy, happiness, peace, and love; they need an opportunity to shine again.

There are so many individuals who have been put on the no-good list, the used-up list, the down and out list, the throw away list because they have been broken by their circumstances and things beyond their control.

Some have made mistakes; some have fallen on challenging times causing them to lose all hope. Instead of other people seeing the value that still exist in them they cast them aside or just throw them away. Others need to realize that there is still potential in that individual just like items in a second chance store; they too only need to be given a do-over.

Once a vase of mine was damaged, it was shattered into so many pieces until the most logical thing to do with the pieces were to discard them. The vase wasn't expensive but held sentimental value to me because it was given to me by a friend. So, instead of throwing it away, painstakingly the pieces were glued back together. You could see the lines in the vase where the glue was applied, but it didn't matter because it still was able to serve the purpose it was made for. That vase was made to hold a beautiful bouquet of flowers and the cracks that evidenced it had been broken, did not deter its use.

God is a God of a second chance; He cares for us; therefore, He cleans us up and gives us the opportunity to start over again when we have messed up or made mistakes; and that second chance is ours for the asking. The scars of our brokenness may or may not be visible, but either way they will not hinder us from serving the purpose we were created for.

One cannot let the scars of the past visible or hidden, whether physical or mental prohibit them from living up to their full potential. That's why we must turn our brokenness over to God.

Jeremiah recounts the Lord telling him to go down to the potter's house to receive a message from Him. **Jeremiah 8:3** reads "*So I went down to the potter's house, and I saw him working at the wheel. But the pot he was shaping from the clay was marred in his hands; so, the potter formed it into another pot, shaping it as seemed best to him*". *(NIV)* The potter did not throw the marred vessel away, he simply made it over again.

God will do the same thing for his people if we ask Him to. He will shape us into the person He wants us to be. And if our brokenness is the result of unrepentant sin, he reminds us of these words found in **1ˢᵗ John 1:9** "*if we confess our sins, God is faithful and just to forgive us our sins and to cleanse us from all unrighteousness. (NIV)*

For me it was an exciting and joyous day when my eyes were open spiritually and illuminated to see God's love that existed between, He and His creation and to be cognitive of the fact that His love was extended to a once sinner like me.

At a low point in my life, it was good to discover that even when some of my friends and families had tossed me to the side because of my past, God picked me up, dusted me off and used me for His purpose. That purpose being to spread the news that indeed God looks beyond our faults and sees the needs of those who put their trust in Him. I am so grateful that I am a witness to this truth.

Because God is not a respecter of persons what He has done for me and so many others who were in the same predicament as I was, "lost", He will do for others, all who ask to be made clean. It does not matter how debased one may have become because of their past, God can still use them.

It is hoped that you the reader will grasp from this book the love God has for His creation and see that because of that love He does not want to see anyone perish, therefore He continues to give persons second chances.

God gives second chances regardless of how many mistakes persons have made, how low they may have sunk and no matter how others may feel about them if that person comes to him in sincerity, with a broken and contrite heart.

A broken and contrite heart is a heart that experiences godly sorrow and exhibits sincere remorse, filled with a sense of guilt, and eagerly desires atonement for past sins and mistakes. Remembering those sins and mistakes causes a person to repent and a repentant heart God will not despise.

If you need a second chance, be encouraged because God sees you and He sees your worth.

Preface

This book is the result of the time and effort put into writing and preparing a sermon for a special program hosted by one of the local churches in the area where I reside. Although prepared for that one occasion, the message has been preached to many congregations some local and some in faraway areas.

Contrary to what some people may think preparing a sermon takes a lot of time, studying and meditating.

In getting together a sermon the preacher, teacher, evangelist, or speaker when they exegesis the scriptures, own mind is drawn back to so many things that has happened in their lives; things that relates to the sermon. Because it is impossible to write or speak every thought that comes to mind, one must weed out some things to save time yet get the message across.

When the message is delivered to the people, they only get a mini version of a sermon.

This book gives you a glimpse of a sermon from start to finish and shows how complicated the process is. The focus of any sermon is to explain what the preacher or speaker is saying and show how what is being said or has been said can be applied to those listening lives.

This book is about 5 women in the Bible who are held in high honor, but after much research about them it was discovered that they were women who could have been placed in a class with women who were considered from the Red-Light District, yet God chose to use them; God chose to give them a second chance, even though to some they may have been considered damaged goods.

Before discussing the five women whom the message is built around, you will read about the lives of other women in the Bible, each with their own personality and coming from diverse backgrounds.

You are at an advantage than the person sitting in church or in an assembly listening to a sermon, because in reading this book you get the unabridged version of a sermon you get a message that has not been diluted to save time.

You get an opportunity to read and reread a line, a paragraph, or a whole page until you get the full meaning of what the speaker is saying.

Reading a sermon gives insight in the type of person the speaker is for bits and pieces of their own lives are hidden between the lines of what they have written.

Each preacher, teacher, evangelist, and clergy person have their own way of putting a message together. Some use stories, some pull on their own life experiences, and some rely on the Holy Spirit as their guide. But no matter how the message is put together or delivered, drawing the congregation in so that they can hear whom the message is about, "God, Christ and the Holy Spirit" and not get caught up in the speaker's own rhetoric is the most important thing.

When first called into the ministry, most of my preaching a sermon was done from memory without writing anything down but getting older requires more than preaching from memory; therefore, cheat cards are always in front of me to keep me on track.

Some people say that reading from or referring to notes is not preaching at all only reading, however, that's not true. Written or given from memory, the words are inspired by God. And God's words according to **Isaiah 55:11**, *will not return unto Him void, but will accomplish the purpose for which God has sent it.*

The Bible is the inspired word of God: God spoke, someone wrote, and we have what Paul says is scripture that is *"God-breathed and is useful for teaching rebuking, correcting, and training in righteousness".* **2ⁿᵈ Timothy 3:16** *NIV.*

It is with much gratitude and thankfulness to God for the incentive to write down my messages and thoughts and when those writings are revisiting it is as if God is speaking to me all over again.

In reading a sermon there is also an aspect of that sermon that the reader is not privy to, and that is the many times the writer has put words in and taken words out to make the message as clear as possible. Even in the rewriting there are still things that the writer misses, such as a misspelled word, a punctuation mark out of place or some other mistake, after all the writer is not perfect; nobody is and that my friend is the whole thought that is conveyed in this book. Nobody is perfect yet God has a plan for each of our lives.

So, sit back in your favorite easy chair, or curl up on your sofa and listen to what the preacher has to say. In doing so you might just be intrigued by how the preacher's mind works. You may also get a unique eye-opening experience from what is written and a different perspective about some of the things in the Bible you have heard over the years.

Acknowledgments

I want to express my sincere appreciation to those pastors and congregation who gave me the opportunity to preach this message at their church. I realize that at first the subject matter of the sermon and even the title itself could have been controversial to some, however you listened.

It is hoped that after hearing the message you were enlightened just as much as I was enlightened when preparing it.

In all things we are to give God glory, and I glorify God and pray that if the heart of one person who thinks they are of no use to anyone, can be drawn to God, and see their worth, then the time and effort put into this work is not in vain.

I do believe that God will provide an increase in whichever way the increase is needed; whether, financially, spiritually, mentally, of physically. And so, everything is left in His mighty hands. With a prayerful heart it is hoped that He does a work, in me, in you, and all who dare to read this book.

Jeremiah 29:11 NIV
*For I know the plans I have for you," declares
the* L<small>ORD</small>*, "plans to prosper you and not to harm
you, plans to give you hope and a future.*

Women from the Red-Light District

Who Were in God's Plans of salvation

Chapter 1

Thrifting

What is your favorite pass-time? Mine is going to flea markets and yard sales. This new generation calls this pass time **thrifting.** In laymen terms, for those not familiar with this new way of shopping, thrifting means carousing at a thrift store, garage sale, yard sale or flea market where you will find used items at discounted prices. These items have been loved by a previous owner, but now they have no use for them and decide to do away with them cheap. Usually, the items are in decent shape with enough life left to them to be useful to someone else.

Everybody loves a bargain and why pay a dollar for something when you can get it for a dime? That is why on any given Saturday you can find me browsing through other people's yards, houses, barns, or storage building, anywhere a sign is posted stating there is a sale going on, hoping to find that certain item that captivates my attention, engrossing me until living without it would be to my detriment.

Thrifting has now become my first choice before shopping at the large department stores.

Beside saving money, giving new life to old things gives me so much joy and satisfaction. Things that one person can no longer see the value in or do not have any use for can be brought back to life and fit a whole new purpose for someone else. A little cleaning, a couple of cans of spray paint can rejuvenate any item. The old idiom, *"one man's trash is another man's treasure"* holds true to me.

Then there is always the possibility of finding that special item that will take a person from living from paycheck to paycheck to living a life dreamed of by many, the life of a millionaire.

Haven't you heard of persons who have stumbled onto a rare and valuable piece at a yard sale or thrift market? They purchased the piece because the color caught their attention or because it was different and unusually, only to later discover it was a rare treasure. It may have been a vase by Rene Lalique, a piece of jewelry by Tiffany, a painting by Vincent Van Gogh, or some other item and because the person brought it their whole life has changed.

Discovering anything of immense value at a yard sale, anything that would make me rich that is, has not happened to me yet, but there is always the possibility, so I keep thrifting. But mostly, the thrill of the hunt is what excites me.

My sister works in health care, and she once replied to me, "Sis you are as clean as the state board of health." Whenever there was a chance that the state was coming in to inspect the facility where she and others worked, extra effort was given to make sure that everything was neat and clean, as to avoid getting a bad grade. When she made that statement, she meant her "sis" was clean, and she liked the outfit. Little did she know that the outfit was a yard sale find that had been put in the hands of a reputable dry cleaners and now looked brand new.

On another occasion someone asked me, "where did you get your outfit" and my reply was "It's old and has hung in the closet for years until where it came from eludes my memory," not wanting to disclose that it was picked up from a yard sale. But now since everyone is thrifting, it is no longer necessary to keep my favorite place to shop a secret. There are persons whose coffers are filled with more than what will ever fill mine shopping at these bargain places.

Thrifting has become so popular now, until you don't have to leave home to do it, for the internet is filled with on-line thrift stores. Many persons sell their personal goods from their homes on eBay, amazon, or their own websites. If you are looking for a bargain now that bargain is just one, click away.

Chapter 2

The Red Lamp

Over thirty or more years ago I recall going to a yard sale with one of my best friends. This friend has long since passed, and her passing grieves me even to this day. Each time thoughts of her invade my mind my heart is permeated with sadness and joy at the same time. Sadness because we can no longer enjoy our days of exploring together, and joy because she is gone to a better place. She had such a wit about her and some of the crazy things she would say, not to mention her humorous antics brings a smile across my face when reminded of them. She always had a way of keeping me in stitches, even when experiencing a difficult day.

On this day we were browsing the local yard sales and at one sale a lamp caught my attention. The price was right, it was only a dollar, so to let this bargain slip through my hands would be foolish. The little table in front of my bedroom window was the perfect place for this little treasure.

Holding the lamp in my hand and saying to my friend "look at this." She looked at me sideways and said, "I know you are not going to buy that lamp." Stunned by her response my reply was why not; it is only a dollar? It was then that she said, "but it's a red lamp." Still naïve, coming back at her with "what is wrong with red"? "You know that empty table in my bedroom needs something on it, this lamp will be the ideal addition". That is when she explained to me, that a red light was what the ladies of the night, prostitutes, and such use to tell their potential customers they are available. She said I just want you to know what you are setting yourself up for, not to mention the talk you will get from the neighbors. She did not have to tell me a second time, for after that moment of schoolings, that was one bargain that was left behind.

For years we had many laughs about that incident. She would always say to me "if you could have seen the look on your face; and how quickly you put the lamp back." Totally embarrassed would have been an understatement.

Thinking about that red lamp struck up my curiosity about the woman having the sale; was that what she used the lamp for, did she no longer need it because she had given up that profession, so many question crossed my mind. This woman was being judged without me knowing anything about her; appearances can be deceiving and sometimes a person's curiosity can cause them to make the wrong assumptions about other people. Just as quickly as those inquisitive thoughts came up, they were vanquished from my mind just as quickly.

My friend knew that I grew up in the country and was never exposed to some of the things that occur in the big cities, so she was always looking out for me.

It's good to have someone who will be honest with you and keep you on track; that's what good friends do.

Chapter 3

Days of Innocence

No longer is the country my place of abode where, as children the only excitement we had was running to catch the milk cow that had broken out of the fence or scrambling to put the pigs back in their pen when they got out. You would not believe how fast farm animals can run when they do not want to be caught. "Like a greased pig" probably originated from someone trying to catch their pigs that had broken out of the pen.

Those days of innocence are gone, and, in some ways, they are missed. Country living was a simpler yet peaceful life. However, being young and when living at home as children, we longed for the fast pace of city dwelling, and vowed when we grew up, we were leaving the country for good.

Hearing about all that transpires in the city made us anxious to the point that we could not wait to experience it for ourselves. But now after leaving the country, getting older and reading about and seeing the violence that takes place in the big city and hearing the noise that accompanies being a part of that environment, makes one long for the solitude that the country offers.

A person does not realize just how close to nature they are when residing in the country. To hear the birds chirping early in the morning and watching the sun as it so radiantly beams through the trees and to be able to feel the cool breeze coming through the bedroom window that has been left open all night, presented a peace that was unexplainable.

We seldom closed the windows or locked the doors in the country because no one bothered things that did not belong to them. However, now, whether in the city or country, everything is bolted and locked each time a person leaves home and especially before retiring to bed at night. My how times have changed.

A part of growing up, becoming mature awakens a person to the hard truth that the world is comprised of all kinds of people; the good, the bad, and even the ugly. Living in the country where we were sheltered from most of the cities' unpleasantness and experiencing mostly good, leaves a person vulnerable; but thank God for friends who keep persons like me in check.

When my friend mentioned the prostitutes and ladies of the night, her comments caught me off guard. To hear of women and sometimes men, who engage in prostitution would have been unheard of in the country. Even if there were those who engaged in this type of activity it was never talked about.

Myself along with my eight siblings lived a very sheltered life, my father made sure of that, therefore, we were never exposed to certain thing and certain talk. Dad even regulated what we watched on television. And when our parents talked to each other when there were things that they did not want us to hear, they talked in a way that we could not understand. Isn't it funny how adults talk in code when there is something they do not want the children to hear or understand? But thinking about it now, that is the way children talk today when they don't want adults to know what they are talking about.

Once my mother acquired a book, recovered from the trash where it had been tossed by one of the ladies she cleaned for. The book had to have been very interesting because mother read it all day. When my father came home from work, she began to whisper to him about what she had read in the book. As she told him about the book, he became furious, and ordered her not to read it again and to get rid of it. We did not hear what she said, regarding the content of the book, but do remember my father asking her where she got the book. From his demeanor we assumed it could not have been biblically based.

Although only a child, my curiosity was aroused about what the book could have been about but dared not ask any questions. One can only assume that it was a topic that my father did not want my mother exposed to let alone us children.

Mother was a fair skinned lady and loved her red lipstick, because red exemplified her already luscious lips, she wore it so good, but this would infuriate my father. Red brought out the best in my mother but the worst in my father and I often wondered why. Perhaps it had to do with how men viewed women who wore red.

11

But no matter how our parents tried to keep us from being exposed to life's unpleasantness, we sometimes stumbled on some of them unexpectedly.

Our country home sat on five acres of land and nearby was a body of water we referred to as a creek. That creek was how the township we lived in got its name, Green Creek.

On any given occasion me and my other siblings would go fishing in that old creek or pick blackberries that grew on the edge of it. Looking back on those times we waded in those murky waters it is evident that we were acting precariously and can see now how dangerous it was. It can be assumed now, but we didn't think about it then that the water moccasins and other undesirable creatures found the water just as inviting as we did. Our parents knew the danger, and perhaps that was the reason we were told to steer clear of it.

One morning after momma and daddy had gone to work, we decided to go for an excursion at the creek just to play in the water for it was a sweltering summer day. As we got to the entrance of the creek, we noticed a car parked with two people inside. Being curious we approached the car and discovered the two in the car were our neighbors. One neighbor was a female, she lived alone about a half mile from our house and the other neighbor a male who lived with his wife and kids about two miles from where we lived.

It was not until sometime later that we discovered we had interrupted one of their rendezvous. It was no wonder the man greeted us with a cheapest grin and asked what we were doing down at the creek? A more poignant question would have been to ask him what were the two of them doing down there together, but as mentioned earlier, we were so naïve and did not have the sense to put two and two together.

It goes without saying that just like we interrupted them, they interrupted our playtime at the creek, however, it was probably for the best.

We could not tell our parents about the incident because we were not even supposed to be at the creek. Imagine how hard it was for us as children to keep that secret. If we could have told what we had seen, we would have confirmed a lot of the gossip that was going on during that time.

So many things have changed since we were children living near that creek. Recently passing by that way revealed that a large steel gate had been placed at the entrance to keep people out.

Gone are those days of innocence, for living life in general teaches a person a lot of things some of which they do not really want to know.

$Chapter\ 4$

Ladies of the Night

Life has taught me that in every large city there is a section of that city that persons should avoid going into, especially at night. And if they do go at night they do not need to go alone. These are the places known as the **"Red Light District"'** where women of ill-repute, prostitutes, and ladies of the night hangout looking for potential clients.

These people are dressed in enticing attire, sporting fancy hairdos, and wearing a lot of makeup. Some wear their fishnet hose and mile high-heel shoes. Usually, they can be spotted at first glance. And then there are those engaged in such activity who look like regular everyday people, and one would not suspect them to be involved in such profession.

Persons who sell themselves for money feel as if this is their only way of making a living and since the money is good, they are unwilling to give this type of lifestyle up.

This lifestyle has put many persons through college, paid for food and rent when other employment was not available. If you were to ask any of the persons engaged in prostitution, why they chose such a profession, they would ask "what's wrong with it" the same as I did about the red lamp.

Then there are those who engage in prostitution not for the money at all but are like me when it comes to "thrifting," they enjoy the thrill of the hunt.

The behavior and actions of those who have taken up this lifestyle are looked upon as deplorable by Christians and without a doubt they have condemned such person to hell's punishment for choosing to exploit themselves this way.

However, if persons would do research on their own family tree or do research on the family tree of those who condemn person who engage in prostitution, they would discover that many of their ancestors played the harlot or acted like a prostitute. This can be substantiated when you see who they are related to.

The older folks had a saying that was often heard when growing up that said, "there's a snake on the line." While the meaning of that old saying was never really divulged to me, it was assumed it meant that some sneaking around had been going on. But again, some things are not talked about.

One thing that that has become evident over the years and that is before a person marries, they need to check out their family tree for there is a possibility that you could be dating or courting your kin. Family secrets are like leaves on a tree, too numerous to count.

Leaves on a family tree are ancestors that a person shares DNA with. All it takes is a puff of wind to shake those family secrets loose, the same as leaves on a tree, and all will know whose has been sleeping with who.

Sometimes Christians often expound on the good and never deal with the bad or unfavorable. The same way we never talked about prostitution and such behavior when growing up, is the same way some people avoid talking about subjects considered taboo today.

Sexual exploitation has been going on ever since man was created. The blues singers like "Johnnie Taylor" and the "Blues Brothers" sang about it in their songs. They asked the question "who has been making love to your old lady while you are out making love? The answer to that question is you would be surprised.

Even when it comes to expounding on the biblical scriptures persons tend to highlight the lives of the good characters, and slightly mention the bad, but almost never expound on the downright evil.

So, when approached about speaking at a Women's Day program for a local church the incident with the red lamp was immediately brought back to my remembrance because of the color chosen by the women and the theme for the occasion. Red was the color the women had chosen, and the theme was "Covered by the Blood."

How could an appropriate yet soul stirring message be gathered from the information given? The message would not come from me, but through the guidance of the Holy Spirit.

John 14:26 reminded me that at the right time the Helper, the Holy Spirit would teach me and bring everything needed for the message back to my remembrance. Therefore, it was assumed that the Spirit of God prompted me to think about the incident with the red lamp.

Since God knows everything, perhaps that day at the yard sale when my attention was drawn to that red lamp, that was God's way of preparing me for this speaking engagement. Although it would be many years later before coming into the ministry, God knew what laid ahead further down the road; he knew His plans for me better than I did.

Even the courses taken when attending college, makes it obvious to me now that God was preparing me.

Having taken a public speaking course and remembering the teachers' words helped me produce the title for the sermon that was being prepared. The instructor said, "know your audience and grab their attention with your first words or opening statement." It is important to note that the public speaking award in the class was given to me that year.

When preparing the message for this speaking engagement, there had to be a catchy subject something that would get the attention of the congregation, draw them in and hold them, so the message was titled "Women from the Red-Light District." The subtopic "Who Were in God's Plan of Salvation" came later after my research had been concluded. This title was sure to make an impact on the women and even cause the men that would be in attendance to sit up and take notice.

It was assumed that the congregation would know what the red-light district was, but for clarity when the day came to speak a more detailed definition would need to be given. So, the message would begin by giving the meaning of red-light district.

Red-light district sometimes referred to as the pleasure district, is a part of an urban area where a concentration of prostitution and sex-oriented businesses, such as sex shops, strip clubs, and adult theaters, are found. In most cases, red-light districts are particularly associated with female street prostitution, though in some cities, these areas may coincide with spaces of male prostitution and gay venues. Areas in many big cities around the world have acquired an international reputation as red-light districts.

The term *red-light district* originates from the red lights that were used as signs for brothels. This definition made it clear to me why my friend so vehemently objected to my purchasing that red lamp from the yard sale.

After reading the definition for red-light district it was concluded that it would take a daring person to use this subject to address a group of church people. How could a preacher approach such a topic? What would the congregation think of me and what would be the starting point of such message? This was a subject that had to be expounded on very cautiously, thereby relying on the Holy Spirit for guidance was paramount.

Although the bible is filled with persons considered to be from the red-light district, they were considered evil and very seldom were evil persons expounded on openly.

There would be some present who would be turned off by the title of the message thinking it would be provocative and X rated, however, we are to never judge a book by its cover or a message by its title.

There would also be some listening to the message that might assume from the title or subject that it would be one that would criticize or condemn a certain group of people, again that would not be the message intent.

And still there would be those presence who would think the message was about them; thinking someone had leaked their business to the preacher or singled them out because of their past lifestyle.

None of these would be the purpose of the message. First it was hoped that the message would show that things are not always as they seem and for that reason one must keep an open mind about everything even when reading the Bible.

Matthew 7:1 tells us this, *"judge not that ye be not judged."* KJV

The most important reasons why we should not judge other people is because often we lack adequate information. We must make sure that we have all the facts. More times than not we judge a person or situation without knowing the entire story. That is why it is important not to judge until we know all there is to know about a person or their situation.

For instance, my purchasing the lamp at the yard sale that day would have been solely to fill a need, which was to occupy a vacant spot on a table. It would also have been used for the purpose it was made, to give light and not used as a means of soliciting clients for acts of prostitution. However, persons who did not know me would read more into a red lamp in my window, than its intended purpose, therefore it pays to get to know people before assuming the worst about them. The same thing applies with biblical characters, we must get to know them, before forming an opinion about them also.

Secondly it was hoped that the message spoken would show how God can turn bad circumstances and those we call bad people around so they will work for His good.

Seated in the congregation would be some sanctimonious persons who would be quick to condemn those persons labeled as bad, especially those persons who were prostitutes, ladies of the night, and other labels given to this group of individuals, however, God can choose to use anyone to fulfill His intended purpose, for He knows the plans He has for each of us.

Dr. Martin Luther King Jr. once said "There is some good in the worst of us and some evil in the best of us. When we discover this, we are less prone to hate our enemies." If we take the time to get to know a person, then perhaps we can understand why they do the things they do.

I am sure everyone at one time or another has assumed the worst about someone, only later to discover that your assumptions were wrong. Your assumptions were based on what you thought you knew rather than what the truth of the matter was, and after you were aware of

Chapter 5

Preparing for the Message

Since this was a Women's Day speaking engagement, developing the sermon required studying many women in the Bible, those mentioned in both the Old and New Testaments.

During my research on some of the women in the Bible, it was discovered that some of them had names, and some were un-named. However, all the women were equally important to ensure a vivid picture could be formed of women's influence in biblical history.

Reading about each woman and studying their history it became necessary for me to place them in certain categories; the good, the bad, and the evil. Those categories were based on the behavior of each woman studied.

Remembering my early years growing up there were just a few women who expounded on the word of God, because it was reinforced repeatedly that women were not supposed to preach, therefore the roll of the woman in the Bible came from a male perspective. On the rare occasions when women were mentioned even if they had impeccable reputations, in the sermons delivered by the men, those women were portrayed in a negative way. Some of the male preachers managed to discredit any woman and although they were not bad, made them seem that way. Very seldom did they give any credit to the women who had done good.

For instance, we would hear sermons where the downfall of man was always placed on Eve. I recall hearing messages that contained these words "if it wasn't for Eve, Adam would have never eaten the forbidden fruit." Another preacher vehemently exclaimed that all the worlds' ills were because of Eve. One preacher in another sermon used the subject "Don't fall for a Delilah" always adding a hint of dry humor to the message.

It was not until women began to put their spirit-led insight into preaching the word of God, that we came to realize that Eve did not force Adam to eat the forbidden fruit, he ate of his own free will and if Samson had been obedient to his parents, he would have never gotten involved with Delilah. Samson disobeyed his parents and gave in to the lust that was in his heart. No one can make you do anything that is not in your heart to do, good or bad, each one of us has a choice.

You would think that since we are living in the twenty-first century that men would move past such sexist idealism, and attitudes about women but some have not. It was not too long ago that the acceptance of a speaking engagement at a church reiterated to me that some males' thoughts regarding women never change, they only see them as sex objects.

The occasion was for a women's day program and involved being down right insulted by the preacher of the church. Although not addressing me, but the women in his congregation he made the statement "you women look good, almost good enough to take to **"China Town."**

China Town, exclaiming to myself. My head dropped and my heart sank, where did that come? It was unbelievable that a man of the cloth would make such a comment to any woman let alone members of his own congregation. It was this type of dry humor that women have been subjected to in church and other places for years. The women in his congregation acted as if his comments did not phase them; could it be that they were used to such comments, or perhaps they did not know about "China Town."

"China Town" is a section of a city where an ethnic enclave of Chinese located outside of mainland China, Hongkong, Macau, Singapore or Taiwan, have settled, most often in an urban setting. While this section of the city is known for its restaurants, and other businesses, it has also become known for its houses of prostitution and sex trade. There is a China Town in big cities such as New York, San Francisco, Boston, Philadelphia, and almost all the larger cities.

The preacher could have been referring to the women looking good enough to take to a restaurant but to me he was saying they looked good enough to be peddled off at a sex shop. If that was the way his comments were discerned to me, they probably were discerned that way to others. It was just an inappropriate and degrading statement. He should have said the women looked good and left it at that and kept his other comments to himself.

Had the preacher made such comments now, because of the "Me Too Movement" his comments could have landed him in hot water. The nerve of that preacher, "China Town".

It goes without saying that his comments shook me, but God delivered a word that day. Guess what the subject of that message was, how ironic; "Women from the Red-Light District". After the message I am sure God revealed to him that woman or any person who is looked upon in a negative way, does have value.

If the preacher had the mindset and viewed the women of his congregation or others as only sex objects, he learned that they can still be used by God, if they are in God's plans.

Had it not been for the spirit's leading he would have never been corrected for his demeaning comments; and it was done not by me but by the word of God. It takes the word of God to dispel some of the beliefs that some individuals have harbored over the years.

In studying the lives of some of the women in the Bible we get a glimpse of all types of women. Some are strong, some beautiful, some vindictive, some God fearing, and the list goes on and on. It was discovered that these women personalities and characteristics vary just as much as the colors in the rainbow.

While all the women in the Bible led colorful lives typically, when we have women day festivities, we gather information on and talk about those women in the Bible who were highly esteemed, honorable, and prestigious. Women such as Queen Esther, Lydia, Dorcas, Deborah,

Ruth, Naomi, Hannah, Peninnah, and Mary to name a few; these are the main characters that are usually expounded on.

Admittedly, it would have been so easy to compose a sermon from the list of women mentioned above, for many church goers are familiar with them, however, it would have been difficult for me to fit them into the color scheme chosen by the women for their day's festivities and to tie them to the subject.

When the names of the women that were just mentioned and others in the Bible are recalled each of them do remind me of a color, however the first colors they bring to mind are not red.

Let us look at the lives of some of these women for their lives and actions cause us to reflect on our own lives and ponder how we would react if faced with some of the dilemmas they were face with.

Chapter 6

Queen Esther

When the name Queen Esther is mentioned, she could be associated with purple because that color denotes royalty. Queen Esther is said to have been an incredibly beautiful woman who became the queen when the Persian king Ahasuerus sought a new wife because his former wife Queen Vashti refused to exploit herself in front of the king's men.

The king wanted his wife to dance in front of his men exposing herself for them to drool over and admire her beauty. Vashti's refusal to obey his order angered the King and he allowed some of the men in his court to talk him into denouncing his wife.

The king needed someone to take Vashti place, and after many days of preparation Queen Esther was summoned to the king and she found favor with him. Esther later used her beauty and the favor she established with the king to save her people the (Jews) from annihilation. Yes, Esther was a Jew, but she kept that a secret.

What an interesting message could be derived from the life and works of Esther, especially the most quoted line from the book named after her "Esther"; Esther said, "If I perish, I perish."

In a world where so many people's primary concern is self, it causes one to wonder how many people today would be willing to risk their own life to save someone else?

It took a lot of persuasion from Mordecai, Esther's uncle to get her to go in unto the king without him summoning her. He convinced her to do so by reminding her that she was also a Jew and perhaps that is the reason she was elevated to her position as Queen, to save her people. Mordecai reminded Esther that if the other Jews perished, she would also.

All too often when persons receive honor and recognition, they forget from whence they came; and that is not a good thing.

Do you remember those in your past who helped you? Speaking for myself, quite a few names come to mind who encouraged, me and they will never be forgotten.

Some are still alive, and some have passed on, but when they cross my mind, my heart is filled with gratitude for them taking the time to instill in me words of wisdom that I can pull from even today.

Wisdom is one's knowledge of what is true and real, one's good judgement, and the ability to learn from one's experiences and mistakes.

In Proverbs 8 wisdom is portrayed as a woman who calls people to learn her ways and find life.

It was the wisdom of Esther that alerted the king to the plot of Haman against the Jews.

God's purpose was accomplished through Esther in the perilous time that she lived in.

Chapter 7

Lydia

Another woman in the Bible that has been the subject of many Women Day programs is Lydia.

When the name Lydia is mentioned, she is associated with purple also, because the Bible says she was a seller of purple. Lydia was a businessperson in the city of Thyatira and a woman of wealth. Lydia knew her business well, she was highly skilled in working with the dyes and textiles.

She was the first convert of Paul to Christianity in Europe. Lydia's house is said to later have become the site of the church in Philippi.

Lydia showed hospitality to Paul and his ministry, and this was a testament to how courageous she was. Her actions of having a group of foreign men stay in her house could have caused a scandal, thus ruining her reputation not to mention her business also. But she risked it all in the furtherance of the gospel, and to be a witness of Jesus, Christ.

When no men could be found seeking the gospel Paul went unto the women and they gladly received him, and his teachings about the Messiah.

In **Matthew 19:27,29** NIV Peter replied to Jesus *"We have left everything to follow you! What then will there be for us?" Jesus said to him, "Truly I tell you, in the renewal of all things, when the Son of Man sits on His glorious throne, you who have followed Me will also sit on twelve thrones, judging the twelve tribes of Israel."*

What are you willing to risk for the sake of the gospel of Jesus Christ, our Lord, and Savior? Would you risk your good name if it meant ensuring that the gospel message goes forth?

William Shakespeare uses the phrase "What's in a name" in his play Romeo and Juliet. He goes on to say "that which we call a rose by any other name would smell as sweet" and Maya Angelou said "They may forget your name, but they will never forget how you made them feel"

I believe both Shakespeare and Maya Angelou were saying that the name isn't as important as deeds the person does. Only the things that we do for Christ will have a lasting impact on our lives and the lives of others. A person acts on what's in the heart not their name.

Chapter 8

Deborah

Deborah is associated with brown because she was a woman who was down to earth. Deborah was a prophetess and the fourth judge of pre-monarchic Israel. We read about her in the book of Judges. She is the only female judge mentioned in the Bible.

Deborah was a woman of wisdom, revelation, and discernment.

She was instrumental in inspiring the Israelites to a mighty victory over their Canaanites oppressors.

It was after Deborah consented to go into battle with Barak that he agreed to fight against Jabin's army.

Deborah, however, was upfront with Barak and told him that victory would be at the hands of a woman. Jael, the wife of Heber the Kenite, subdued and killed Jabin, thus making what Deborah had said come true.

Deborah was not concerned with prestige or making a reputation for herself, she was just being obedient to God.

Would you have done what she did, risk life and limb, knowing that you would not be given credit for doing so?

Deborah realized that being obedient to God far outweighs the honor that one receives from humankind. Humans will make you a hero today and be ready to put your head on a chopping block tomorrow if you cross them.

That's why Peter replied, *"I'd rather obey God than man."*

When we are obedient to God, we hear him when He speaks, we trust the things He tell us to do, and we willingly surrender to Him.

Obedience to God demonstrates the faith that we have in Him, and we trust Him wholeheartedly. We do so not expecting to receive anything in return, but we do so because it is the right thing to do.

God promises us that if we are obedient, He'll save us, protect us, and provide for us.

Deborah knew she could count on God and that is why she was obedient to Him.

Chapter 9

Dorcas

Dorcas who is sometimes referred to as Tabitha was a woman held in high esteem by those who knew her. She was called a disciple of Jesus and we find mention of her in the book of Acts.

Dorcas lived in Joppa and is known for her good works and acts of mercy. She was a widow and Dorcas can be associated with gold because of a halo many have placed on her head, describing her as a saint.

One day Dorcas died, and the people sent for Peter to come. She was later raised to life again, but nothing else is mentioned of her after that.

The life of Dorcas teaches us to do good while we are alive, always putting the needs of others before self. If we do this then we will be remembered by the ones we have done good to, and by God.

How will you be remembered?

Will your eulogy say that you were one of the selfless persons that anyone has ever known, or will it say the opposite?

Our lives will one day come to an end but the good we do remains.

Chapter 10

Hannah

Hannah reminds me of blue, because she was always down in the dumps until God blessed her with a son. Hannah is mentioned in 1ˢᵗ Samuel and was one of the wives of a man named Elkanah.

The Bible says Hannah was barren. Her husband loved her, but to carry on his family name, he needed someone to give him children, when Hannah could not Elkanah married another woman.

Elkanah's second wife made life unbearable for Hannah, but when Hannah had enough of being harassed by Elkanah's second wife, she prayed to God for a child and God granted her petition.

In time, Hannah had a male child, Samuel. Later she gave the child back to the Lord just like she had promised and subsequently had other children.

Hannah's son Samuel became a great judge and prophet who loved and obeyed God.

Samuel was born because Hannah prayed and believed in Prayer.

Could you have taken the abuse that Hannah took? Do you believe in the power of Prayer to the extent that you were willing to wait like Hannah for your prayers to be answered?

All too often when circumstances turn out different than what we envision, we are prompted to take matters into our own hands, rather than wait for God to bring a resolve to our problems. When we go ahead of God, we usually end up making a mess of the whole situation. But if we trust God, He will work things out for our good.

That is what Hannah did; she prayed and trusted God and things worked out in her favor.

Chapter 11

Peninnah

One can hardly think of Hannah without thinking of Peninnah also.

Peninnah can be associated with green because she was so envious of Hannah. She too is mentioned in 1st Samuel. Although she was Elkanah's other wife who bore him children, she knew that her husband loved Hannah more. Jealousy causes people to harass the person they are jealous of.

It does not pay to harass, intimidate, of belittle anyone, because what goes around comes back around again.

Although not much is mentioned about Peninnah, she was punished because of her actions toward Hannah. That punishment came through the death of her children after Hannah's children were born.

Hannah did not pray for anything to happen to Peninnah or her children, but it happened this way according to the Midrash: Hannah had one child and Peninnah buried two; Hannah bore four children and Peninnah buried eight. When Peninnah knew that Hannah was pregnant with her fifth child, Peninnah feared she would lose her last two sons, so she apologized to Hannah and asked her to pray to God that her last two sons not be killed. Hannah did as Peninnah asked, God granted Hannah what she had asked and Peninnah sons lived, but they were reckoned as belonging to Hannah.

Be careful who you mistreat because Karma is sometimes hard to swallow.

Has there ever been a time when you had to forgive someone who had wronged you? I am sure that most of us can say yes, because if you are a Christian, it is the Christian thing to do. We are reminded of our responsibility to forgive in the "Model Prayer" that Jesus taught his disciples.

Matthew 6:14 *For if you forgive men their trespasses, your heavenly Father will also forgive you.*

Chapter 12

Mary

There were many women in the Bible named Mary, but the color that comes to mind with Mary is light yellow simply because of the spikenard, or oil that one of the Mary's used from her Alabaster box to anoint the feet of Jesus.

While there were those who complained that Mary wasted this costly ointment, Jesus accepted her gift and spoke these words to her naysayers *"leave her alone for she has done an excellent work on me."*

When others disapprove of what we do, not knowing our reason for doing them, may we ask if what we are doing is pleasing to God although it may be displeasing to others. If God is pleased, then all is well.

All was well with Mary because she did not let the sneering and idol talk hinder her from doing what she had to do.

What Mary did was not done on a whim, she did not know it at the time, but this would be the only anointing that Jesus would receive prior to his death. As the bible tells us, when the women went to the tomb to anoint Jesus' body after his crucifixion, he had risen.

If the spirit moves you to act, do so for the spirit knows better than we.

Is God happy with your words, actions, and deeds? As for me I pray that He is.

Have you ever done something that others did not understand, or even at the time you did it you did not understand, but later God revealed to you that what you did was orchestrated by Him?

That's the way God works, because His thoughts are not like our thoughts nor His ways like our ways; His ways are higher than ours and His thoughts better than ours.

Mary understood what she had to do, and she did it.

Chapter 13

The Virgin Mary

And when the name Virgin Mary is mentioned, she reminds me of white, because she was as pure as the driven snow.

It is only logical that Mary was chosen to be the one to birth our Lord and Savior, for just as she was pure, so was he.

There is much to be said about Mary the mother of Jesus, however she will be discussed in greater detail as we continue to put this sermon together.

Four of the eight women listed above could be characterized as being from the red-light districts because of their actions. **Esther** was bathed and pampered so that she would find favor with the king. What does the word favor mean? It means approval, support, or liking, etc. The king chose Esther because of her beauty; however, it was the king's lust for her that really put Esther in the place she needed to be. We can only imagine what transpired in the king's chambers.

God is not mentioned in this book, but we can see God's providence working to accomplish His plan. God can use anyone for His purpose and He had His reasons for allowing Esther to become Queen. Yes, Esther acted like a Harlot, but she did what she had to do, she did what God allowed her to do. She saved her people the Jews from annihilation.

Lydia's house to some could have been construed as a house of ill-repute instead of a house for the worship of God. What would you assume if you see a group of foreign men going in and out of a single woman's home? I am sure you would assume the worst, that the woman was running a brothel. Things are not necessary the way they look. But we cannot control how other people's minds think.

Peninnah enjoyed her encounters with Hannah's husband so much so until she kept making Hannah's life miserable. Peninnah failed to realize that she was the second wife-concubine, who bore Elkanah children. Today we would call her the surrogate, she carried another man's child, however that child was not conceived by artificially insemination. She lent her body as a means for Hannah's husband to carry on his name. Isn't that what prostitution is, allowing one's body to be used for one reason or another?

Mary is mentioned with these other women who could be considered from the red-light district only because so many writings have suggested that she was a prostitute. But even at that Jesus came to her defense when Judas exclaimed that the ointment, she used to anoint Jesus' feet was a waste.

Although these women are listed among the women who are looked up to, there are some questionable behaviors that would lead one to think that they are less than perfect. Again, it depends on how you look at things.

Chapter 14

Some Bad Women in the Bible

There are other women in the Bible who are not so honorable and revered as the women we just discussed; rarely do people discuss these women especially at gatherings such as Women's Day Festivities. However, their names need to be mentioned and discussed because by including their names in the discussions it shows that the Bible is filled with persons who have good qualities and bad qualities. Often in our preaching we only talk about the good and this gives a one -sided view about persons who comprise bible history.

The so-called bad women led colorful lives also and when their names are called, they can be associated with a color; each of them can be identified with the color red. Although they can be associated with red, they were not the type women to use to inspire a group of church women, however it is worthwhile to mentioned them briefly.

A Woman with Power-Jezebel

One woman that comes to mind that is considered bad is Jezebel. The word of God describes Jezebel as being the wickedest woman that ever lived. She was a worshipper of Baal. Not only was she wicked, but she enticed her husband to do wicked.

In **1ˢᵗ Kings 21:1-25** we find out that she had a man killed to get his land for her husband, King Ahab. Not only that she sought to kill one of God's prophets by the name of Elijah. But in the end Jezebel got what was coming to her.

The word power means possession of control, authority, or influence over others. The ability to act or produce an effect.

Jezebel had power but used her power for evil, to bring harm to someone else. She used her power to fulfill a desire of her husband. Jezebel's power was also used to keep her husband under her influence. Jezebel had so much influence over her husband, until she persuaded him to forsake his God, the one true God, and turn to the worship of Baal, an idol of Jezebel and her followers. When she was threatened with the loss of her power by the Prophet Elijah, she sought to have him killed. With God on Elijah's side, he prevailed, and the prophesies made about Jezebel came to pass. She was thrown from a high window and eaten by the dogs. The only thing that was left of her were her hands. The hands that once had so much power were now powerless.

Proverbs 6:16-19 reads, *"there are six things which the Lord hates, seven which are an abomination unto him: Haughty eyes, a lying tongue, and hands that shed innocent blood; A heart that devise the wicked purposes, Feet that are swift in running to mischief, A false witness that uttered lies, and he that soweth discord among brethren"*

Red is the color associated with Jezebel because red symbolizes **POWER.** Jezebel had power but she used it for the wrong reason. She used her hands to shed innocent blood.

If you had power, what would you use that power to do? Would you use it for good or for bad? Would you use it for self or for the benefit of someone else?

A Woman with Power in this 21ˢᵗ Century

Stacey Adams

A modern-day woman with power who used her power constructively is Stacey Adams.

Stacey Abrams was born December 9, 1973. She is an American Politian, lawyer, voting rights activist, and author who served in the Georgia House of Representatives from 2007 to 2017, serving as minority leader from 2011 to 2017. Stacey is a member of the Democratic party.

She is listed among the one hundred most powerful women in the world, she ranks #100. Stacey Abrams is the founder of the Fair Fight, a voting rights organization based in Georgia. During the 2020 election this

Chapter 15

An Angry Women, Athaliah

Another woman in the Bible who we rarely talk about is Athaliah. Athaliah was the daughter of Jezebel, and I guess in this case the old saying like mother like daughter is true. Athaliah was an angry woman. She came from a family with money, and power, yet they were not the most popular people around.

Athaliah had a son who became king of Judah, and she was his counselor to do wickedly. Her son subsequently was killed and because of her anger, Athaliah destroyed all the royal seed of the house of David except Jehoash. If the people had not hidden Jehoash, he would have been killed also. Jehoash later became king fulfilling God's promise to David that from his lineage would come the Savior of the world.

Anger is a strong feeling of annoyance, displeasure, or hostility.

It has been stated that Athaliah grew up in a family with power and money, but it is evident that the family was lacking something, and that something was Love.

Athaliah thought that she could take whatever she wanted just like her mother Jezebel took Naboth's land for her father. But upon learning that she had been outsmarted she was moved to anger, so much so until she destroyed many innocent people. Like her mother, Athaliah got what was coming to her also; she was captured and executed.

The color used to describe Athaliah is red. Among other things, red symbolizes **ANGER.**

Proverbs 29:11 *tells us that "Fools vent their anger, but the wise quietly hold it back."* This scripture does not mean that the wise bury their anger or do not deal with it, but it means that they control their anger and how they express it. When you restrain your anger, you keep it within limits.

Anger can be used in a positive way if we allow our anger to motivate us to bring about change for the better. Do you have any unresolved anger in you? Has that anger prompted you to act in a negative way toward someone or something?

Have you learned how to quietly hold back your anger, if so, you are wise, however if you have not Solomon says in Proverbs 29:11 that you are foolish.

Seeing that Solomon was the richest and wisest man that lived, accept, and trust his assessments regarding anger.

Chapter 16

A Dangerous Woman-Potiphar's Wife

Another woman we rarely discuss is a woman who has no name of her own. She is simply referred to as Potiphar's wife. She is the woman who ran after Joseph, in other words she tried to seduce him. When Joseph did not give in to her advances, she told a lie on him and said that he tried to attack her. This woman wanted what she wanted and was not going to settle for no. When Joseph refused her, she became enraged. A woman scorned is trouble.

The actions of Potiphar's wife remind me of the movie "Fatal Attraction" directed by Adrian Lyne. The screenplay was written by James Dearden. The main characters were Michael Douglas, Glenn Close and Anne Archer. The film centered on a married man who has a weekend affair with a woman who refuses to allow it to end and becomes obsessed with him.

Potiphar's wife was obsessed with Joseph; however, Joseph did not give in to Potiphar's wife. Nonetheless Joseph was marred by this woman's actions and false accusations, but later he came out on top.

Danger means the possibility of suffering harm or injury. The possibility of something unwelcome or unpleasant.

The color associated with Potiphar's wife is red. Red symbolizes **DANGER.**

Proverbs 22:3 3 *The wise see danger ahead and avoid it, but fools keep going and get into trouble.*

Are you living a dangerous life?

Chapter 17

A Vengeful Woman- Herodias

Herodias was a princess of the Herodian dynasty of Judaea during the time of the Roman Empire. She was married to Herod II who she later divorced and married Herod Antipas, the brother to her first husband, Herodias's uncle. When John the Baptist condemned her marriage, she sought a way to get vengeance on him and did so with the help of her daughter Salome. Salome was summoned to dance at Herod Antipas's birthday party and if he were pleased with her performance, she could ask him for anything. Salome pleased the king and when she was asked what she wanted, Herodias told Salome what to ask for "the head of John the Baptist on a platter." The King had no choice but to honor his word.

Herodias hated John the Baptist for speaking out against her marriage to Herod Antipas because she had a living husband. She used her own daughter to get revenge on him.

Red is the color associated with Herodias because it symbolizes **Rage.**

Rage is excessive anger that is often violent. It is best described as a fit of violent anger and fury. It is the most extreme expression of anger. Rage can drive someone to attack someone physically. It can make someone destroy property and rage can drive a person to hurt other people emotionally.

Herodias was despicable because she used her own daughter to execute the rage inside of her against the man who dared to expose her illicit and incestuous marriage.

It was understandable for Herodias to be upset with John, but to use her own daughter as a ploy for her revenge was beyond reprehensible; not what one would expect from a parent.

These are just a few of the women in the Bible referred to as being bad; they had bad personalities, bad dispositions, and often used bad judgement when dealing with people.

If either one of these bad women had repented God would have forgiven them, because that is the kind of God He is. In all my reading and studying of these women it has never been said that they turned from their wicked ways, and perhaps that is why they are rarely mentioned in sermons today.

A sermon could be prepared from what has been disclosed about the lives of each of these bad women of the Bible; Jezebel, Athaliah, Potiphar's wife and Herodias, that would go along with the color the women chose, but neither of these women's lives would fit into the theme. **"Covered under the Blood"** Although most of them did shed much blood.

It was concluded that these four women would not be suitable characters to build this women's day message around, therefore another way to connect the Women's Day color to the theme had to be sought.

Upon further meditation the spirit of God led me to the book of Matthew where the genealogy of Jesus Christ our Savior, is listed.

In times past, reading Matthew chapter one would always cause frustration because of my inability to pronounce the names of all the persons connected to Jesus. However, reading this pericope, there among the long list of men in Jesus' bloodline were the names of five women that caught my attention, who had never been noticed or caught my attention before.

Why did Matthew include these women in his writings? Only the writer himself knows the answer to that question; everything else would-be presumptions and speculations, admittedly there were quite a few of them.

However, studying each of these women it was discovered each had a story of their own, each woman different and unique in their own way, but they also had much in common.

Chapter 18

Genealogy is the study of family origin and history.

These five women whose bloodline could be traced to our Lord and Savior Jesus the Christ would be the women used in the sermon that was being prepared for this speaking engagement.

Since they were in Jesus' bloodline, they would automatically tie into the subject the women had chosen for their special day, "Covered under the Blood" but, how could these women be associated with the message title which would also be the subject, **Women from the Red-Light District?**

One would assume that since these five women are included in Christ's genealogy, they would be women with spotless reputations, and certainly not women we would think would be involved in a profession that is condemned by saint.

However, after studying and researching these five women listed in Jesus' genealogy, it was discovered that their lives were not beyond reproach.

It is hard to believe that in the Bloodline of Jesus, Christ, our Savior that there were women who could be associated with Ladies of the Night, Ladies of ill repute, Harlots, and prostitutes, but there they were, right there in black and white.

Now that the women who would be used in the message were revealed, the subject of the message was formed and the color all tied together, it was now time to assemble the sermon.

The names of the women included in Jesus' genealogy are **Tamar, Rehab, Ruth**, **Bathsheba**, and **Mary**. To build the foundation of the sermon, a deeper look into each of the women backgrounds were necessary.

Making sure that my facts were right was important, because I dared not put such a taboo title on women whom we all have placed on a pedestal because they were in Christ's bloodline without having proof. Therefore, looking deeper into each of their backgrounds and lives was crucial. It was that research which substantiated that each woman could very well be classified as being from the red-light district.

Let us read on.

Family Tree

Chapter 19

Women in the Genealogy of Jesus Christ

Tamar: Genesis 38

Tamar was the name of two unique women in the Bible found in the Old Testament. The one who could have been considered to have been from the red-light district is Tamar, Judah's daughter-in-law. Her first husband was Er, Judah's oldest son. Er died because he was wicked. Tamar later married Onan, Er's brother, Judah's middle son. According to the Old Testament writings found in Deuteronomy 25 this was permitted when the deceased brother has not had a son.

However, when Onan lay with Tamar, he spilled his seed on the ground to keep from giving Tamar a child, this displeased God and Onan died also. Judah promised Tamar to his youngest son, but he never gave him to her. Deep down Judah blamed Tamar for the death of his two sons, so he never had the intention of giving his baby boy Shelah to Tamar.

Tamar knew this so she thought of a plan to get back at Judah. She heard that Judah was going to Enain to sheer sheep, so she dressed up like a harlot or prostitute and sat along the roadside. Judah's wife had died, and he was vulnerable. So, as he passed by Tamar, he could not resist her. He propositioned Tamar, lay with her not knowing she was his daughter-in-law. Months later word came to Judah that Tamar had played the harlot and was with child, so Judah ordered Tamar killed. However, Tamar had proof that Judah was the father of her unborn child.

Tamar had Judah's staff, seal, and cord which he had given her on the night of their encounter; this proof was indisputable, and Judah let Tamar live. Tamar had twins Pharez and Zerah and their birth is recorded in this manner.

Genesis 38:27-30 NIV *When the time came for her to give birth, there were twin boys in her womb. As she was giving birth, one of them put out his hand; so, the midwife took a scarlet thread and tied it on his wrist and said, "This one came out first." But when he drew back his hand, his brother came out, and she said, "So this is how you have broken out!" And he was named Pharez. Then his brother, who had the scarlet thread on his wrist, came out. And he was named Zerah.*

Tamar could be considered a woman from the red-light district because of the way she went about getting Judah to lay with her. The word of God tells us that she dressed up like a harlot and quite naturally that is what Judah thought she was.

Although this may have only happened one time Tamar used her body to get back at her father-in-law, she used her body to get what she wanted. Isn't that what a prostitute does; they use their body for gain.

If Tamar never played the role of a harlot again, the time that she did fulfill the plan God had for her.

Further studying the life of Tamar, it was learned how Pharez one of Tamar's twins played a role in the birth of Jesus.

This shows that even a woman from the Red-Light District can be used and blessed by God. Not because of the good in them, but because of God's grace and the power of repentance.

Isn't it amazing how people can see the fault in someone else and fail to see their own faults and shortcomings? Judah was ready to have Tamar killed, burned to death; to him she was no good. But he discovered that he was just as much at fault in her playing the harlot as she was.

If Tamar had not had proof of who the father of her unborn child was, she would have been killed.

What lesson can we learn from Tamar? We see that as a woman make sure you get some proof!

The attitude of many men in an affair, or illicit relationship is wham, bam, thank you ma'am. Once they have gotten what they want they are quick to push the woman to the side and go on to the next vulnerable victim, leaving each one broken and scarred, and in some instances ashamed. It is in those low times of their lives that these women must realize that all is not lost. They must understand that even in their brokenness that God is a forgiving God, they only need to ask for that forgiveness.

Was what Tamar did right or wrong, who is to say? However right or wrong we must remember that it was all in God's plans, and **God had a plan for Tamar.**

A Modern-Day Woman Who Had Proof

Monica Lewinsky

In 1998 a former White House Intern had the proof she needed to affirm that an affair between herself and the president at that time took place. The intern's name was Monica Lewinsky, and the president was Bill Clinton. His famous statement was "I did not have sexual relations with that woman." Lewinsky's proof was a blue dress with the sperm of the accused man. In the case with Tamar and Monica Lewinsky, the evidence does not lie.

Family Tree

Chapter 20

Rehab: Joshua 6

Another woman who was from the red-light district is Rehab. Rehab lived in Jericho on the city wall a place reserved for people who did not deserve to dwell near respectable residents.

Joshua who has been given the responsibility of leading the Israelites to the Promise Land after the death of Moses, sends spies to search out the land that God has given them.

The spies sent by Joshua turn into Rehab the harlot's house. Her house was positioned on the margins of the city, which allowed Joshua's spies easy access to her as a source of information and collusion.

One might ask was information what the spies were seeking from Rehab or were they seeking something else? Was it because it was easy to access Rehab's house that they chose to turn into her, or was it because of a red light in her window that drew them to her house? Were the spies looking for more than information?

The king of Jericho hears about the spies being in town and he sends men to find them. They go to Rehab, and she lies and says the spies went out the city gate, and if they hurried, they could catch them.

After the two spies left, Rehab goes up on the roof, lifts the flax and brings the spies out. She tells the spies sent by Joshua "I know that God has given you this land and that you will eventually take the city." She asks the two spies for a favor; imagine that a woman who is used to turning favor for men, now ask these two men for a favor.

What did Rehab want? She asked the men when they take the city to spare her father, mother, brothers, and all in her father's household. The spies agree and tells Rehab to bring her family into her house and tie a red cord in the window.

When the onlookers gazed upon the red cord in Rehab's window, they probably thought it was a means of signaling her clients, or a way for them to leave her house or brothel after their rendezvous was over. But that red cord would be the key to saving her and her family's life. Rehab left the red cord in her window to save herself and her family. That red cord is symbolic of the red blood on the doorways of the Hebrew slaves in Egypt. When the Angel of Death passed over the houses with blood on the doorpost the families within were safe.

On the day that Joshua and his men took the city, they marched around the walls of Jericho six times and on the seventh time the walls came tumbling down, however Rehab and her family were spared because of the red cord in the window.

Rehab and her family lived outside the Israelite camp until they were sanctified according to the law of Moses then they were brought into the Israelite's camp. Rehab was indeed a woman from the red-light district, for the scriptures makes that perfectly clear however, her lifestyle did not negate the fact that she cared for her family, and she exhibited how much love she had for them for asking their lives to be spared. When the time came, she joined with the ones who had spared her, and her family's lives. **God had a plan for Rehab.**

Family Tree

Chapter 21

Ruth: Book of Ruth

Another woman in the genealogy of Jesus, Christ is Ruth. Ruth was the daughter-in-law of Naomi. Ruth was a foreigner, a Moabite who had married Naomi's son when Naomi and her husband settled in Moab during the famine. Naomi' husband died and both her sons, leaving her with two daughters-in-laws. Naomi decides to go back to her homeland. She tells Ruth and Oprah to go back to their father's house. Oprah returned but Ruth refused, she went with Naomi back to her homeland and declared that Naomi's people would be her people.

Ruth found favor in the eyes of a relative of Naomi, whose name was Boaz. Boaz treated Ruth with kindness and subsequently marries her.

Ruth and Boaz's marriage originated from their mysterious encounter at the threshing floor. Naomi instructed Ruth to meet Boaz at the threshing floor, explaining: **Ruth 3:1** *"Daughter, I must seek security for you, where you may be happy"*. Naomi told Ruth to bathe, anoint herself, dress up and go down to the threshing floor; do not disclose yourself to the man until he has finished eating and drinking. When he lies down, note the place where he lies down, and go over and uncover his feet and lie down"

Naomi was preparing Ruth for an illicit and clandestine meeting with Boaz. She assumed that Boaz, after eating and drinking, would be unable to restrain himself upon discovering a beautiful woman all bathed, and smelling sweet lying at his feet in the middle of the night, with nobody around to witness the event.

Isn't that what the prostitutes and harlots do? They spend time preparing themselves for the one they are enticing.

Boaz did not touch Ruth that night, but he did later marry her. Ruth's actions if had been made known to the others could have given her a reputation as a woman from the red-light district. But **God had a plan for Ruth.**

Family Tree

Chapter 22

Bathsheba: 2nd Samuel 11:3

Another woman who could be considered from the red-light district is Bathsheba. Bathsheba was the wife of Uriah. Uriah was off at war. One day David observed Bathsheba bathing from the roof top. David sent for Bathsheba laid with her and sent her back home. Word came to David that Bathsheba was with child.

To cover up what he had done, David sent for Uriah, Bathsheba's husband to come home from war. He devised schemes to get him to be with his wife, so he would think the child she was carrying was his, however, his plans did not work so David had Uriah killed. After a period of mourning, David sent for Bathsheba to be his wife.

God sent the prophet Nathan to David to reprove him, he did so by telling a story of a man with one little ewe lamb and another man with many sheep. When the man with many sheep had company come to his house instead of killing and dressing one of his many sheep, he took the one little ewe lamb belonging to the other man; he took all the man had. The one little ewe lamb was Bathsheba, and the many sheep were the wives and concubines belonging to David.

Whether willingly or unwillingly, Bathsheba's actions could be viewed as the actions of a woman from the red-light district. Was she aware that David was eyeing her from the roof top as she bathed? Did she add to his desire for her as she stroked her body with the washcloth and poured water on herself to rinse the soap away? Did Bathsheba enjoy the attention and flirted with David appearing to do so innocently?

As Nathan points out David's sins, he attributes them all to David and Bathsheba bears no blame, so we go by the word of God.

The first child Bathsheba bore where David was the father died, as punishment for David's sin, however she subsequently had another son, Solomon who rose to the kingship after the death of David.

God had a plan for Bathsheba.

Chapter 23

Making the Connection

What would be your assessment of the actions of each of the four ladies just mentioned if you did not know who they were and that they were in the bloodline of Jesus?

Often, we are too quick to give up on people because they make mistakes, they make wrong choices, but we must remember that God is able to turn situations and circumstances around and use them for His glory.

Let us take a moment for personal reflections. As you look back over your life did you make mistakes; did you do some things that you now regret? Sure, you did. Each of us has. God saw fit to pick you up and turn you around, why can't he do it for somebody else, even a woman from the red-light district?

Sometimes as Christians we can be the most judgmental, looking on others with disdain and reproach forgetting that if it were not for the grace of God, we would all be on our way to hell. For the scripture tells us *"For all have sinned and fall short of the glory of God".* **Romans 3:23 NIV**

God knew that some of us were going to be living in the red-light district, but he sent Jesus into the world to die for the sins of the world. And God's son came through women from the Red-light district.

Without knowing their history, you like myself thought that each of the women in the genealogy of Jesus the Christ had impeccable reputations, but now you see they did not. Neither of them was beyond reproach, because each of them acted in a way contrary to how a holy and reputable person should behave. But nonetheless God had a plan for each of them.

Although they had questionable reputations, God used them for His purpose and that purpose was to bring forth Jesus, Christ our Savior.

God used these women from the Red-Light District to fulfill the promise that from David's lineage would come the Savior of the world.

There are persons who assert that the most famous Red-Light Districts exist in places such as Tokyo, Shinjuku, Paton, Singapore, and others. Europe has its share of Red-Light Districts in places such as De Wallen, Amsterdam, the Netherlands, Paris, and France. They also exist in both North and South America in places such as the Dominican Republic, Mexico, Nevada, and others. To some the sex trade has become a way of life and you don't have to look far to find persons engaged in this trade.

How likely would a person think that there are those who could be classified as being from the Red-Light District listed among the names of the women in Jesus' bloodline? Only a few because they have not been told the whole truth, nor have they searched out the truth for themselves.

Just like persons in our family who have bad reputations are not talked about is the same way that the truth about some of the Holy women in the Bible are obscured or hidden; we only talk about the good and omit the bad.

Is it a misnomer to refer to these women as being from the Red-Light District? Some may answer yes, but the action of each woman speaks louder than words.

Now let us look at how each of these women mentioned line up in Jesus' bloodline.

Chapter 24

The Genealogy of Jesus
the Messiah NIV

Matthew 1:1-17

This is the genealogy of Jesus the Messiah the son of David, the son of Abraham:Abraham was the father of Isaac, Isaac the father of Jacob, Jacob the father of Judah and his brothers, Judah the father of Perez and Zerah, whose mother was **Tamar***, Perez the father of Hezron, Hezron the father of Ram, Ram the father of Amminadab, Amminadab the father of Nahshon Nahshon the father of Salmon, Salmon the father of Boaz, whose mother was* **Rehab** *Boaz the father of Obed, whose mother was* **Ruth***, Obed the father of Jesse, and Jesse the father of King David. David was the father of Solomon, whose mother had been Uriah's wife, (***Bathsheba** *added for clarity), Solomon the father of Rehoboam, Rehoboam the father of Abijah, Abijah the father of Asa, Asa the father of Jehoshaphat, Jehoshaphat the father of Jehoram, Jehoram the father of Uzziah, Uzziah the father of Jotham, Jotham the father of Ahaz, Ahaz the father of Hezekiah, Hezekiah the father* *of Manasseh, Manasseh the father of Amon, Amon the father of Josiah, and Josiah the father of Jeconiah, and his brothers at the time of the exile to Babylon. After the exile to Babylon: Jeconiah was the father of Shealtiel, and Shealtiel the father Zerubbabel, Zerubbabel the father of Abihud, Abihud the father of Eliakim, Eliakim the father of Astor, Astor the father of Zadok, Zadok the father of Akim, Akim the father of Elihud, Elihud the father of Eleazar, Eleazar the father of Matthau, Matthau the father of Jacob, and Jacob the father of Joseph, the husband of Mary, and Mary was the mother of Jesus who is called the Messiah. Thus, there were fourteen generations in all from Abraham to David, fourteen from David to the exile to Babylon, and fourteen from the exile to the Messiah.*

The names in bold are the names we previously discussed.

Tamar the woman who played the harlot with Judah had twins Pharez and Zerah. Pharez begat Hezron, Hezron begat Ram, Ram begat Amminadab and Amminadab begat Nahshon, and Nashon begat Salmon.

Salmon married **Rehab** the once prostitute from Jericho, and they had a son named Boaz.

Boaz married **Ruth** the women who acted like a prostitute down at the threshing floor and they had a son named Obed. Obed had a son named Jesse and Jesse had a son named David who became king.

King David had a son by **Bathsheba**, the wife of Uriah's who played the harlot with David and that son's name was Solomon. And after some more begetting here comes the **Virgin Mary,** who gave birth to our Lord and Savior Jesus Christ.

God had a plan for Tamar, Rehab, Ruth, Bathsheba, and Mary. And the plans He had for them led to His ultimate Plan of Salvation, the birth our Lord and Savior, Jesus, Christ.

Chapter 25

The Prophesy of Christ's Birth Foretold

Isaiah 7:14 NIV

Isaiah prophesied that a pure young woman would give birth to God's son. *Therefore, the Lord himself will give you a sign: The virgin will conceive and give birth to a son and will call him Immanuel.* That virgin was Mary.

Virgin means a person who has never had sexual intercourse.

Matthew 1:18-23 NIV

This is how the birth of Jesus the Messiah came about. His mother Mary was pledged to be married to Joseph, but before they came together, she was found to be pregnant through the Holy Spirit. Because Joseph her husband was faithful to the law, and he did not want to expose her to public disgrace, he had in mind to divorce her quietly.

Mary is the name of the fifth woman listed in Jesus' genealogy.

It was said that the Virgin Mary is associated with the color white, because she was as pure as the driven snow, but the spirit of God showed me, that no matter how pure you may be, no matter how good you may be, no matter how innocent you may be, there will always be somebody who is ready to find fault in you and to throw shade at you.

You see there are some who associate Mary as being from the Red-light district, because she became pregnant while she was espoused to Joseph. In fact, Joseph thought that she had been unfaithful, and he was ready to put her away quietly as to not make a public spectacle of her. But an angel of the Lord explained to Him that the child Mary was carrying was conceived by the Holy Spirit and Mary was still a virgin.

Quite naturally, those persons who are not believers, who do not understand the power of the Holy Spirit, do not believe nor accept how the Holy Spirit works. Some theologians have asserted that a virgin cannot bear a child, however faith teaches us that with God nothing is impossible.

Mary conceived or became pregnant by the "Power of God" through the spoken word, the same as He spoke the heavens and earth into being. Mary received what was spoken to her, she believed what was spoken to her, and it was done unto her.

Can you imagine the talk that surrounded Mary's pregnancy? Can you imagine the whispering and looks she received from the other women? However, Mary did not let the rumors and idle talk stop her from carrying the Christ Child. According to **Luke 1:38** Mary said, to the angel, *"I am the Lord's, servant be it unto me according to thy word."*

In other words, Mary was willing to endure the whispering, the shaming, that came along with her consenting to be used of the Lord.

Anytime a person accepts the calling God has on their life, and when they decide to be a servant for the Lord, there will always be somebody ready to talk about what you used to do, what you used to be, but one cannot worry about the talk. Just remember if God can use a woman from the red-light district, or someone thought to be from the red-light district he can surely use you.

God is a forgiving God and we read repeatedly of the instances He forgave women with bad reputations.

The fact that some have the wrong opinion about Mary demonstrates that when persons do not know the whole story, they can assume anything.

Chapter 26

Forgiveness

Forgiveness is a conscious deliberated decision to let go of feelings of resentment or vengeance toward someone else or a group of people who have done you wrong.

Forgiveness, according to the Bible is correctly understood as God's promise not to count our sins against us which is dependent upon our forgiving others.

When we think about forgiveness, it should remind us of the love that Jesus had for humankind that he was willing to lay down his life for us.

Romans 5:8 is a testament of the love that God has for us. *"But God proves his love for us in this: while we were still sinners, Christ died for us".* NIV

Those persons who ask God for forgiveness of their sins and accepts Jesus into their lives and hearts are forgiven of past sins because they are "Covered by the Blood of Jesus".

Asking for forgiveness comes after a person has been made aware of their wrongdoings, has regret for those wrongdoings and vow not to do those wrongdoings again.

As we search the scriptures, we are told of many instances when Jesus chose to forgive women from the red-light district other than the women in his bloodline. Lets' look at a few of them and allow what you read speak to your heart. Put yourself in each of these women's place.

Jesus Forgives Women Who We're from The Red-Light District

Chapter 27

Jesus forgives the Woman at the well.

John 4:26 Then Jesus declared, *"I, the one speaking to you am he."* NIV

John Chapter 4

In the fourth chapter of the book of John, Jesus encounters a Samaritan woman at a well. Jesus holds a conversation with this woman which went against tradition because Jews and Samaritans had no dealings with each other.

An in-depth look at the woman's living arrangements and prior activities suggest that she could be regarded as a woman from the red-light district. In verse seventeen of the fourth chapter of John Jesus says to the woman "go call your husband and come back." She replies, "I have no husband." Jesus follows up with these words "you are right when you say you have no husband, the fact is, you have had five husbands, and the man you now have is not your husband."

For years, this woman had lived the life of a prostitute. She had been looking for someone to give her life purpose and to fulfill a yearning that she tried to receive from various men.

Not getting what she longed for she moved from one man to the next earning her a reputation of being a loose woman and being shunned by the other women of the city.

She no doubt was ashamed of the label that had been placed on her and that is why she made her way to the well to draw water late in the day so she would not encounter the other women; typically, the other women came early in the morning to draw water.

The other women had labeled this woman a bad woman, a no-good woman, and even harsher names. She was of no importance to them; however, Jesus did not see her as the women of the city saw her. Jesus saw this woman as someone he could use to be a witness for him.

If the other women of the city were so holy, did any of them reach out to this woman to help her find the inner peace and contentment she so desperately needed? Apparently, they found more satisfaction letting this woman be the subject of their whispering and gossiping. It would be safe to assume that not one of the other women of the city ventured to hold a conversation with the woman at the well. But Jesus did.

After dialogue between Jesus and the woman, Jesus introduces himself to her as the long-awaited Messiah. That private conversation between Jesus and the woman made her forget what she had come to the well to get, physical water, H2O: for she got what she really needed, the Spiritual Water that Jesus so freely gives to anyone who desires to receive it.

There is a thirst that exist in each of us, that can only be quenched by the Living Water, which is Jesus Christ.

When the woman received it, she eagerly and exuberantly ran into the town telling all to "come see a man who told me everything that ever I did."

Jesus made himself available to a woman from the red-light district, he did not shun her or pass judgment on her like the other women of the city had done.

The woman's salvation began with Jesus asking the woman at the well for a drink of water and ended with his offering her water, (himself, Living Water). She accepted what Jesus had to offer, forgiveness of her sins and Jesus gave her the freedom to live in the newness of life that comes about because of accepting him as her personal savior.

There were those who probably continued to look down on the woman and judge her by her past sins, however she had now been restored, her past was in the past.

Even if the other women and men seen her as she once was, Jesus saw her as a new creation, one who had been cleaned up and rescued from the throw away list. She was given a second chance, and God will give all those who desire a second chance an opportunity to be made new. Even a woman from the red-light district.

2ⁿᵈ Corinthians 5:17 reads *"Therefore if anyone is in Christ, he is a new creature. Old things have passed away; behold all things become new."*

Isaiah 43:18-19 tells *us "Remember ye not the former things, neither consider the things of old. Behold I make new things"*

Jesus is the one who can make old things new again. Just like an item that has been picked up from a yard sale or a garage sale or a thrift store, he rejuvenates that life and gives it a whole new purpose.

Chapter 28

John chapter 8 Woman Caught in Adultery

John 8:11 *"Neither do I condemn thee: go and sin no more"* NIV

As Jesus was teaching in the temple, the teachers of the law and the Pharisees brought in a woman who had been caught in adultery. Those who brought her in said that she had been caught in the very act. She too was a woman from the red-light district.

Her accusers wanted Jesus to pass judgement on her and said that according to the law, the woman should be stoned. However, Jesus did not hold to their way of thinking, he just stooped down and wrote on the ground. As they continue to question Jesus for a response, he said unto them "ye that is without sin first cast a stone at her." Then Jesus stooped down and continued to write on the ground.

Those who heard began to walk away one at a time, the older ones first. Afterward there were none standing there but Jesus and the woman.

Jesus said to the woman "where are your accusers? Has no one condemned thee?" She replied "no one." Jesus said, "neither do I condemn you go and sin no more."

Jesus forgave this woman from the red-light district even though her punishment according to the law was to be death by stoning.

Once again Jesus looked beyond the faults of this woman caught in adultery and seen what she really needed; an opportunity to be cleaned up and restored.

The men who brought the woman to Jesus seen someone they could use to trap Jesus. Jesus realized that the woman had been used enough. Therefore, he gave her another chance to begin anew.

Yes, she had been tarnished by her reputation, but God was not through with her.

Jesus is the silversmith who can *take away the dross from the silver and produce a vessel for the finer.* Proverbs 25:4 KJV

The blood that Jesus shed on Calvary can make one brand new.

When others are quick to point out our faults and wrongdoings, Jesus chooses to have mercy. Jesus can clean up those who have lost their luster and cause them to shine for him. He extends his mercy even to a woman from the red-light district.

Chapter 29

Luke 7:36-50 A Sinful Woman Anoints Jesus' Feet

Luke 7:48 Then Jesus said to her "Your sins are forgiven." NIV

This is one of my favorite stories in the Bible, one that that has been used repeatedly to build many sermons from.

Jesus points out vividly the attitude that some people harbor about individuals who have sinned, yet not realizing that there is room for improvement in all our lives.

Jesus has been invited to a meal in a Pharisee house by the name of Simon, he accepts the invitation and goes in and reclines at the table.

Then a woman comes up behind him with an alabaster flask of ointment and begins to anoint Jesus' feet with her tears and wipes his feet with her hair and afterward anoints Jesus' feet with the ointment.

It is later disclosed by Simon that the woman is from the red-light district, a prostitute.

Simon holds animosity toward the woman for her lifestyle and finds objection to Jesus allowing her to touch him. Jesus does not agree with Simon's attitude toward the woman and chooses to forgive her because of the outpouring of love she has shown him in the anointing of his feet.

He Publicly says to the Simon according to the NKJ *"Therefore I say to you, her sins, which are many, are forgiven, for she loved much. But to whom little is forgiven, the same loves little."* Then Jesus says to the woman *"Your sins are forgiven."*

Simon thought the woman to be of no importance and considered her defiled. He even murmured to himself if Jesus knew what kind of woman, she was he would not allow her to touch him.

Simon's attitude toward the woman could be compared to the other women's attitude toward the woman at the well and the men's attitude toward the woman caught in adultery; they saw them as sinners needing to be avoided and punished for their wrong doings.

Instead, Jesus thought these women were worth saving because this woman like the other two women had potential.

We can only see the outer appearance, but there is a part of everyone that is hidden from the outside, it is what lies in the heart.

The scripture says, man looks on the outward appearance, but God looks at the heart.

That is why Jesus chooses to forgive. He seen women who were good at heart but had been driven to make some wrong choices by circumstances beyond their control.

Maybe the lifestyle the women were living was not out of pleasure, maybe it was out of a need to survive.

Regardless if we admit it or not, all of us do what we must to survive and go to even greater lengths to survive if we have little children who are depending on us. Our actions and choices might not be right, they may sometimes be degrading, but you do what you must do.

Chapter 30

Why Jesus Forgives

These three women, the woman at the well, the woman caught in adultery and the woman who anoints Jesus each were guilty of being harlots, prostitutes, or women with bad reputations, however Jesus chose to forgive them of their sins, why? The answer is because they needed his forgiveness. They needed a do over, they needed a second chance.

Jesus went to the cross of Cavalry to pay the price for the sins of all. **Hebrews 9:22** NIV states that in fact, *"the law requires that everything be cleansed with blood, and without the shedding of blood there is no forgiveness"*. *NIV*

Another reason Jesus chose to forgive these women was because each of the above women perhaps reminded him of those women that are in his bloodline who had a bad reputation. Although each woman could be labeled as being from the Red-Light District, Jesus knew of the struggles and hardships they had to overcome for God's plan of sending a savior into the world could be accomplished by them. Jesus knew that each of them had a purpose.

How could he not forgive a woman from the red-light district when the women in his bloodline exhibited the same tendencies?

When a person accepts Christ, his blood cleanses them from all unrighteousness, and it was because of the women in his bloodline that Christ was born to serve out the will of his Father; save mankind from their sins so they could be reconciled back to God.

Chapter 31

The Blood of Jesus

The song writer says, what can wash away my sins, nothing but the blood of Jesus. What can make me whole again, nothing but the blood of Jesus. Oh, precious is the flow that makes me white as snow no other fount I know nothing but the blood of Jesus.

Another song writer says the blood that Jesus shed for me, way back on Calvary it will never, lose its power. It reaches to the highest mountain and flows to the lowest valley the blood that gives me strength from day to day, it will never lose its power.

These songs and so many others remind us of the power of the Blood of Jesus.

That is why God sent His son into the world so that all who believe in him and accept him as their savior would have eternal life. We read this in John 3:16 one of the most quoted scriptures in the whole Bible.

John 3:16 reads *"For God so loved the world that he gave his one and only Son, that whoever believes in him shall not perish but have eternal life."* *NIV* Whosoever includes Women from the Red-Light District.

Each of the women that Jesus forgave can be compared to a treasure at a yard sale, thrift store, garage sale or other places where secondhand items are sold.

They were written off as being of no value by someone else. The woman at the well was written off by the other ladies of the city. The woman caught in adultery was written off by the men who caught her. The woman who anointed the feet of Jesus was written off by Simon. But Jesus did not write them off, he knew right where to find them and what it took to restore them to usefulness. Jesus cleaned and polished them up and afterward they had value.

Maybe their value was overlooked by others especially to those who had tossed them aside, but they had value to God. And the good thing about it is that God can do the same thing for you, and you, and whomever feel as if they are damaged beyond repair.

God is the one who can restore all the downtrodden, the lost, and all that are in a sinful state. Once cleansed they can be used to be a light to others whose self-esteem and self-worth has slowly been depleted. God can use them as part of His plan.

God knows how to make us over again.

2ⁿᵈ Corinthians 5-17 is worth mentioning again. *"Therefore, if any man be in Christ, he is a new creature:*

old things are passed away, behold, all things are become new". KJV

Becoming a new creature is a promise that you receive a new lease on life. You can now begin a fresh work of God. In simple words becoming a new creature means you are given a second chance.

Chapter 32

What does your red represent?

Let us recapitulate what has been said this far about red and what red represents:

Red represents power-Jezebel

Red represents anger, -Athaliah

Red represents danger, -Potiphar's Wife

Red represents rage, -Herodias

Red represents the red-light district -Tamar, Rehab, Ruth, Bathsheba, Woman at the well, Woman caught in adultery, Woman who anoints Jesus' feet, and some may infer that Mary the mother of Jesus could be placed in this category too.

But most importantly Red represents the blood of Jesus.

1ˢᵗ John 1:7 *"But if we walk in the light, as he is in the light, we have fellowship one with another, and the blood of Jesus Christ His son cleanses us from all sin". NLT*

It does not matter what your red may have represented in the past, when a person accepts Jesus Christ as their personal Savior red will come to represent that you too are in the bloodline of Jesus because you have been adopted into the family of God.

Being in God's family makes you covered by the blood of Jesus. When you hear that you are **covered by the blood**, it means that your debt of sin has been paid and you are forgiven.

Because of the sins of the first man Adam and the first woman Eve, humankind was separated from God. To restore spiritual life to sinful man, it is only reasonable to demand the life of an acceptable substitute. Jesus Christ, the Savior is the substitute and all who believe in God and accept Jesus as Lord and Savior of their life; all are forgiven of their sins.

Have you been washed in the blood, are You Covered by the Blood?

If your answer is yes then you no longer should feel guilt and shame for past sins, even if your sin was being from the Red-Light District.

I can hear the voice of God say, *"Come now, and let us reason together, saith the Lord: though your sins be as scarlet, they shall be as white as snow; though they be red like crimson, they shall be as wool."* **Isaiah 1: 18. NIV**

Have you been redeemed* by the Blood of the Lamb? If you have then you are a Rare Treasure; you are of great worth and value, you are esteemed as rare or precious

Chapter 33

Redeemed*

The word redeem means to buy back, repurchase, to get or win back: it means to free from distresses or harms: to be free from captivity by payment of ransom.

Throughout this book we have talked about obtaining a second chance, and as we look at the meaning of the word redeem, it becomes apparent that Jesus gave his life as a ransom for all of us. Jesus paid the price to repurchase, buy back win back each of us from the clutches of sin.

One of the greatest examples of what Christ done for humankind is illustrated through the story of Hosea and his wife Gomer.

Chapter 34

Hosea "a prophet of doom" with a message of restoration.

God's love demonstrated through the love a man had for his wife, who was a **Woman from the Red-light District** is the next to last woman who will be referenced in this message, the woman's name is Gomer.

Gomer was a harlot. She was married to Hosea, one of the minor prophets of the Bible. It was not by accident that Hosea married a prostitute or a lady from the red-light district, he knew all about her before he married her.

Hosea was obedient to God and when God told him to take a wife of harlotry, he acted upon what God told him. Although Hosea was good to Gomer, she was not faithful to him, and repeatedly she reverted to her old ways of prostitution.

Gomer left their home and wandered into the arms of other lovers on numerous occasions leaving behind her loving husband and children. It did not matter that they had children together, the children did nothing to ensure her fidelity to Hosea.

Each time Gomer left she always managed to comeback; and of course, Hosea received her back with open arms.

But the last time Gomer left Hosea, she was not allowed to return on her own, she had to be redeemed.

Gomer was being sold into slavery to pay debts that she had incurred. Her only means of making money was the selling of her body.

The only way she could be saved and rescued was by Hosea paying a price so that he could bring his own wife back home.

Reading this story many of you would say "I wouldn't have done it" you would say "good riddance, she got what she deserved" There would be those who would say that she was damaged goods, and not worth the price of redemption. You would just throw her away.

But before you condemn Gomer you must be reminded that this story is an illustration of how Israel had done their one true God; the one that loved them unconditionally. God used Hosea's marriage to illustrate to the people just how unfaithful they had been toward Him.

Hosea represents God and Gomer represents God's people.

The relationship that was to exemplify life between God and His people is outlined in the Ten Commandments: ..." thou shall have no other god before me..." God comes first, and our fidelity is to Him above all other things.

God was good to His chosen people, loving them, providing for them protecting them, but they would continuously run after other gods putting them before the one true God. God's people were unfaithful to Him just like Gomer was unfaithful to Hosea, however, God's love for His chosen people never wavered just like Hosea love for Gomer never did.

This story is a reminder of how many persons today are treating God, they still are putting people, places, and things before Him: sinning through words actions and deeds.

But God is faithful and even in our unfaithfulness, He still pursues us, not wanting any one to perish.

God sent Jesus into the world, to redeem us from our sinful and idolatrous ways, just like Hosea redeemed Gomer from her adulterous ways.

Hosea could not bear seeing his love being sold into slavery although she had done him wrong.

God does not want any of His creation to be slaves to sin, so He sent Jesus into the world to be the propitiation for the sins of the entire world.

It was Jesus who paid the price to buy each of us back from Satan clutches. He paid the price not with silver or gold, or any other material thing, but with the blood of his precious Son Jesus, the Christ.

So, before you condemn the women from the red-light district who has played the harlot repeatedly, or the male from the red-light district, who had done the same, remember that many of us have played the harlot also, we have put so many things ahead of God.

We may not have committed adultery but have committed idolatry and one is just as bad as the other, because there is no little sin or big sin, sin is sin.

But the same way God had a plan for each woman from the red-light district in this book, He also has a plan for you. He can restore you and use you for his glory.

Thank God for the redeeming power of the blood of Jesus, for it is through that precious blood that Jesus shed on calvary that has given me and others like me a second chance.

There was a time when I played the harlot, not in respect to how the word is used in the physically sense, but in the spiritual sense, putting so many things ahead of God. But now without reservations an unapologetically can affirm that my life has been changed and it is all because God gave me a second chance.

Borrowing the words from a song by "Anthony Brown" a gospel recording artist; "God thought I was worth saving so He came and changed my life God thought I was worth keeping so He cleaned me up inside. God thought I was to die for, He sacrificed His life so I could be free so I could be whole so I could tell everyone I know..." I can say that I have been given a second chance.

That is what the word redeems means, being given a second chance.

The one who can give each of us a second chance is Jesus the Christ.

Do you need a second chance? Jesus stands ready to give you that chance, and it is yours for the asking.

Aren't you glad that God chose to not put us on the no-good list, the down and out list, the throw away list, but instead he chooses to put us on the list of possibilities, or future potential list?

None of us can see into the future or predict the future with accuracy, but God can. He knows what we all are destined to become and although some might be headed in the wrong direction, God can quickly change our route.

There's a song that comes to mind that says, "I'm on the right road now." The songwriter was saying that they were on that downward road that was crowded that led to destruction, but by the grace of God, their route was changed, and they got on the road where there is only a traveler every now and then but, in the end, it is that road that leads to eternal life.

Matthew 7:13,14 reads *Enter through the narrow gate. For wide is the gate and broad is the way that leads to destruction, and many enter through it. But small is the gate and narrow the way that leads to life, and only a few find it...*

Because God can change the situation and the person, therefore we should not be hasty in our judgment of others.

Matthew 7:1-4 KJV *Judge not, that ye be not judged. For with what judgment ye judge, ye shall be judged: and with what measure ye mete, it shall be measured to* *you again. ³And why beholdest thou the mote that is in thy brother's eye, but considerest not the beam that is in thine own eye? Or how wilt thou say to thy brother, let me pull out the mote out of thine eye; and behold, a beam is in thine own eye?*

While so many people judge according to what they can see, many persons have been judged unjustly, based on outer appearances.

One of the basic rudiments of life should be to get to know a person before passing judgement or making assumptions about them.

It is not the intent of this message to cause a rumpus, nor is it in anyway condoning acts of prostitution, and such, but it is given to show that primordial attitudes about any group of people is wrong. It is God who has the final say about each of our lives; for prostitutes, ladies of the night, and harlots have hearts too.

To validate this statement, I want us to draw from this last story because it summarizes all that has been said.

Read on.

Chapter 35

A Prostitute Mother's Heart

Samuel 16:7b

The Lord does not see as man sees; for man looks at the outward appearance, but God looks at the heart.

The human heart is an organ that pumps blood throughout the body via the vessels of the circulatory system, supplying oxygen and nutrients to the tissues and removing carbon dioxide and other waste from the body.

In the Bible, the heart is considered the seat of life or strength. In the Bible the heart means mind, soul, spirit, or ones' entire emotional nature and understanding.

The scripture coming from Samuel chapter 16 verse 7 says God looks at the heart; not the organ but He looks at our mind, spirit, our entire emotional nature. If the Lord looks at the heart, then He sees every bruise, every battering, every break our hearts endure. While others may not see beyond our skin and not into our pain, God does. He is aware of our deepest wounds, our greatest needs.... God knows the condition of our hearts at this very moment, and He cares.

The scripture I read was God's response to Samuel when he was sent to Jesse's house to anoint the next king over Israel. Samuel looked at Jesse oldest son and he just knew he was to be the next king, but God rejected him, because he knew what was in that son's heart.

After none of Jesse's sons in the house were to be the king, Samuel asked if there was another son and there was David, the little shepherd boy who was tending his father's flock.

David was the one to be the next king although on the outside he did not look like a king. The Bible says that David was a ruddy looking boy, but God seen beyond what was on the outside he saw his heart and David had a heart after God's own heart.

After the death of Saul, who was the former king of Israel, David became king. Now his reign is ending, he is about to die, and his son Solomon is anointed the next king over Israel.

Solomon was young when he became king. The Bible tells us that Solomon was the richest and the wisest man that ever lived. Solomon had an opportunity to ask anything of the Lord and instead of asking for riches and long life he asked God for wisdom that he may be able to rule over God's people. Because Solomon did not ask for riches God gave them to him anyway.

Then there came a time when Solomon had to decide how to handle a tricky situation; After this incident it was proven to all that the wisdom of God was with Solomon.

Listen closely to this story for the heart of this message comes from it.

Two women who were prostitutes gave birth at about the same time. They lived in a house together. One night one of the women laid on her baby and killed it. When she discovered her baby was dead, she got up from her bed and put her dead baby in the other woman's bed and took the other woman's baby from beside her. When the woman awakens that morning and sees the dead baby, she knew it was not hers. But it was just her word against the other woman.

They took the matter before king Solomon to settle the dispute. Since there was no way to rightly know who the mother of the living child was, Solomon asked that a sword be brought, and the baby be divided in half.

The mother who had made the switch said cut the baby in half if I cannot have the baby, she cannot either. But the real mother said no give the child to her so that the child can live. The real mother knew she had to relinquish her rights to the child to save the child. She could not bear the thought of cutting her child in half.

Although this woman lived a sinful life, and the child may have been conceived in the wrong way the real mother loved the child enough to let the child go.

Solomon said give the child to the one who was willing to let the child live because she is the Real mother.

There are mothers who must let their children go because they are not able to care for them properly, but it does not mean they do not love them. They let them go so that they may live.

They let them go so that they may have enough of the things that the real mother cannot afford to give them. They know that their children deserves so much more so they let them go.

And because we cannot see their hearts, we assume everything is okay with them. However, we cannot see how this hard decision is eating them up inside.

And because some of the ones who give up their children cannot deal with the pain, the heartache and sadness, of relinquishing their child, or children they try to alleviate the pain by turning to superficial means to mask the hurt of their hearts.

And instead of persons showing compassion and trying to do something to alleviate the pain that these persons are going through many have the audacity to judge them, look down on them and criticize them. They just throw them away.

Elvis Presley sang a song that says, "walk a mile in my shoes, walk a mile in my shoes, before you abuse, criticize, and accuse, walk a mile in my shoes". In other words, Elvis was saying you cannot see my heart.

On the outside they may look as if they have it all together, but the loneliness, the guilt, the shame of having to let their children go, is sometimes unbearable.

No none of us can know what is in the heart of another person but there is someone who does and that someone is God. Because God knows and cares he tells us in **Psalm 147:3** that *"He heals the brokenhearted and binds up their wounds."* No matter the source of your heartbreak, God can repair your wounds.

Psalm 34:18 tells us *"The Lord is close to the brokenhearted and saves those who are crushed in spirit."* Though you may feel defeated God is closer than you realize. He is always with you and can heal your heart.

Isaiah 41:10 *"So do not fear, for I am with you; do not be dismayed, for I am your God. I will strengthen you; I will help you; I will uphold you with my righteous hand."* God's love and strength will help you through anything that you are facing.

God loves you! even when you are at your lowest point and you feel as if no one loves you, God loves you.

To know the love of God is priceless.

No, you do not have to resort to superficial means to try and alleviate your pain. What are examples of superficial means: drugs, alcohol, sex, food, gambling among other things.

These superficial means just cover up the hurt for a little while, and when that high is gone, or you sober up the hurt is still there.

God provides a means whereby when a person becomes burden down and they think they cannot go on they can release everything to Him. **1st Peter 5:7** NIV *"He says cast your cares upon me for I cares for you."*

Take your burdens to the Lord and leave them there. If you trust Him and never doubt, He will surely bring you out.

When you accept Jesus as your personal savior you can turn your problems, worries, trials, and tribulations over to him and he will carry them. Jesus says, **Matthew 11:29** NIV *"take my yoke upon you and learn of me for my yoke is easy and my burden is light."*

When you have God on your side and His son Jesus interceding on your behalf you can make it.

God did the opposite of what the mother in Samuel was willing to do. She was willing to give the child away to save the child, but God gave his son away to save us.

This story of the mother that was a prostitute proves that sometimes persons are judged as not caring simply because of mistakes they have made, however God looks beyond the fault and sees what that person really needs.

God sees the hearts of **Women from the Red-light District** and stands ready to forgive them, save them and restore them.

Isn't it ironic that God used a King, Solomon, born from a woman of the red-light district, Bathsheba, to discern the heart of a mother who was a prostitute?

That alone illustrates how God can turn people and situations around, especially when those persons are in His plans.

The good thing about how God can turn a person's life around is He does it without degrading and humiliating them.

There use to be a custom in the "Baptist" denomination, and it might have been practiced in other denominations also, where when a young girl was found in the "family way", she would have to stand in front of the congregation confess her sin and make apologies to the congregation. This seemed so un-fair because the boy was never subjected to such open rebuke.

Many times, the girl would leave the church rather than be the brunt of church gossip. It is good that this is no longer done.

What would have been the attitude of the members of the congregation if they knew that many women in the Bible were guilty of doing the same things that the girls being singled out had done; and some of those women were in Jesus' bloodline.

John: 20:31 reads, *"But these are written, that ye might believe that Jesus is the Christ, the Son of God; and that believing ye might have life through his name."*

John's objective in his writings was to present the facts that others may become believers. He wrote the truth and when we preach, we must preach the truth, the whole truth and nothing but the truth.

If we present the truth as revealed in the word of God, not as we see it, then others will see that God is a forgiving God.

He forgives all who ask for forgiveness.

Chapter 36

The Closing

You have been given insight into how a sermon is put together. You see how complicated the process is and what writing or getting a sermon together encompasses.

These are the components that goes into preparing a sermon:

Praying,

The Topic

Praying

Studying

Praying

Preparing

Praying

Writing

Praying

Rewriting

Praying

Presenting

Praying

All the way through getting the sermon together, we see that prayer is a key component; begin with prayer and end with prayer.

How many of you would imagine that preaching one message could cause so many thoughts, to be brought back to a person's remembrance?

But remember this, no matter how well a sermon is prepared, it is the Holy Spirit that does the work, both in the preaching and in the drawing of those who are being preached to.

In all things God gets the glory!

God has a plan for each of our lives and He can use anyone of us if we are willing to be used by Him and that includes women from the red-light district.

You have been presented with the preacher's thoughts, and research, now it is time to deliver the sermon.

But remember the way the sermon is written does not mean that it will be delivered that way, because who knows what will happen when the Holy Spirit takes over. We must allow the Holy Spirit to have His way, because the Holy Spirit knows who is in the congregation and what each of them need to hear.

Every sermon is not for everybody, but everybody should be able to grasp something from each sermon that is preached.

In **Matthew 11:15** Jesus said *"Ye that have ears to hear, let them hear."* He was calling for people to pay careful attention to what was being said and heed to what you have heard.

The day to deliver the message has arrived and how should you begin. What do you say in your opening and in the sermon. You have so much information to draw from, but you would be in church for hours and hours trying to deliver everything you have put down on paper.

Therefore, you let the Spirit of God lead you.

This is what I was led to say.

Chapter 37

Setting Protocol

Giving honor to God, to the pastor of this church, to the visiting pastors, officers, members saints and friends, it's good to have been invited to share with you on your special day.

You ladies look stunning in your red, and if you had not given me a heads up about what your color for today was, there certainly would have been no problem figuring it out.

Thank you to the Women's Day chairperson for extending an invitation for me to be your speaker. I consider it an honor and a privilege to have been asked to come. You could have asked any woman from a long list of women, more capable than myself, who would have been more than willing to accept the invitation, but you asked me and I am grateful. Also thank you goes out to your wonderful pastor for giving the consent for me to come and give you what the Lord has given me.

The theme you have chosen for this occasion is "Covered by the Blood" and your color red, goes right along with the theme.

For weeks I have pondered, studied, and meditated about a message that would go along with the theme and color you chose, and the spirit led me to the Old Testament, the book of **Isaiah chapter 1:18.** Reading from the KJV of the Bible That pericope reads as follows: *Come now, and let us reason together, saith the LORD: though your sins be as scarlet, they shall be as white as snow; though they be red like crimson, they shall be as wool.*

Let us pray:
Dear God let the words of my mouth and the meditation of my heart be acceptable in thy sight O, Lord my strength and redeemer.

Chapter 38

The Sermon

From the scripture that was just read in your hearing, coming from **Isaiah 1:18** we get this subject: "Women from the Red-Light District, who were in God's plans of Salvation."

The Red-Light District is defined as a part of an urban area where a concentration of prostitution and sex-oriented businesses, such as sex shops, strip clubs, and adult theaters, are found. Those persons who engage in such activities are called prostitutes, harlots, ladies of the night, and other names associated with this profession. Some engage in this profession for money, others for promotions, and still there are those who do so for the thrill.

When we hear of persons who engage in such activities they are frowned upon, talked about, and condemned especially by Christians.

Usually, we judge them without knowing anything about them or their reason for doing what they do.

This message is not given to condone such behavior, nor condemn anyone, but it is given to allow all to see, that:

1. God can use anyone He wishes to fulfill His plans
2. God is a God of a Second Chance
3. We shouldn't judge anyone until their complete story is known.

I know some of you may be insulted because you are wearing red, and you think that you are being put in the category of prostitutes, harlots, or ladies of the night; that is certainly not the case. May I remind you that you picked the color, you chose the theme, however the message comes by way of the Holy Spirit.

The point that I want to make in this message is there are women who are or have been prostitutes, harlots, ladies of ill-repute who are looked down upon as being a nobody. They have been thrown away by friends and families alike and even by some church folk without being given a second thought, let alone a second chance. But God can give them a second chance because God knows the plans, He has for them.

In biblical history there are persons, we esteem highly, but research shows that their lives are not above reproach.

There were many women in the Bible who played the harlot. Some of them are women that we put on a pedestal and the ones that most of the women's day festivities are centered around. However, researching the backgrounds of some of those women that are highly esteemed, research suggest they were not without spot or blemish. But God did not throw them away as many today would do, He used them; why, because through them you received salvation.

Let me explain, it was because of God's plans for these women that Jesus Christ, our Savior was born, and his birth made a way for my and your redemption.

God has a plan for each of us, and if we would allow Him too, He will make His plans known to us. **Jeremiah 29:11** gives us this affirmation: *For I know the plans I have for you," declares the* LORD, *"plans to prosper you and not to harm you, plans to give you hope and a future.*

Have you ever taken a close look at the five women mentioned in Jesus' bloodline? In preparing for this message, I did. The names of the five women listed in Matthew chapter 1 are Tamar, Rehab, Bathsheba, Ruth, and Mary and after studying a little bit about them, it was discovered that four of them acted like women from the Red-Light District and one was thought by some people to have been from the Red-Light District.

There were many other women in the Bible whose lives have been used to build women's day messages around, but the Spirit didn't lead me to use any of them, because God wants all to see that His thoughts are not like ours, nor His ways like ours.

How likely would we associate the women in Jesus' bloodline, as being women defined as prostitutes, harlots, or ladies of the night rarely, but they were. Even if their actions were only done one time, each could be identified as being from the red-light district.

Let me give you a little background on each of these women.

Tamar dressed up like a harlot and sat alongside the road and when her father-in-law, Judah came by, he propositions her, lay with her and she later became pregnant. **Genesis 38:13-16** Extended Bible reads: *When Tamar was told, "Your father-in-law is on his way to Timnah to shear his sheep," she took off her widow's clothes, covered herself with a veil to disguise herself, and then sat down at the entrance to Enaim, which is on the road to Timnah. For she saw that, though Shelah had now grown up, she had not been given to him as his wife.*

When Judah saw her, he thought she was a <u>prostitute</u>, for she had covered her face. Not realizing that she was his daughter-in-law, he went over to her by the roadside and said, "Come now, let me sleep with you."

Rehab was indisputably a harlot because the word of God identifies her as such. Rehab hide the spies that Joshua sent to Jericho to spy out the land. **Joshua 2:1** NIV reads: *Then Joshua's son of Nun secretly sent two spies from Shittim. "Go, look over the land," he said, "especially Jericho." So, they went and entered the house of a <u>prostitute</u> named Rahab and stayed there.* **Joshua 6:25** NIV *And Joshua saved Rahab the <u>harlot</u> alive, and her father's household, and all that she had; and she dwelleth in Israel even unto this day; because she hid the messengers, which Joshua sent to spy out Jericho.*

Bathsheba was the wife of Uriah who lay with King David and became pregnant. She bore a child that later died, and after the death of her husband at the plotting of David, Bathsheba becomes David's wife. **2ⁿᵈ Samuel**

11:4-5 NIV reads: *Then David sent messengers to get her. She came to him, and he slept with her. (Now she was purifying herself from her monthly uncleanness.) Then she went back home. The woman conceived and sent word to David, saying, "I am pregnant."*

Ruth planned an illicit encounter with Boaz down at the threshing floor. Although Boaz didn't touch her, she still acted like a prostitute. **Ruth 3: 3-5** NIV *Wash thyself therefore, and anoint thee, and put thy raiment upon thee, and get thee down to the floor: but make not thyself known unto the man, until he shall have done eating and drinking. And it shall be, when he lieth down, that thou shalt mark the place where he shall lie, and thou shalt go in, and uncover his feet, and lay thee down; and he will tell thee what thou shalt do. And she said unto her, all that thou sayest unto me I will do Naomi was preparing Ruth for an illicit relationship with Boaz.*

She assumed that in Boaz, after eating and drinking, would be unable to restrain himself upon discovering a beautiful woman lying at his feet in the middle of the night, with nobody around to witness anything that may have happened.

Mary has always been viewed by those who are not believers, that Jesus was not conceived by the Holy Spirit and view her as being a harlot because she became pregnant before her, and Joseph consummated their marriage. **Matthew 1:18** NIV *When his mother Mary was engaged to Joseph, before they lived together, she was discovered to be pregnant by the Holy Spirit.*

I believe what the word of God says, what you or anyone else believes is yours and their prerogative. This points to the fact that sometimes what we do not know allows us to make wrong assumptions.

But despite their flaws, mistakes or sins, or what others assumed about them, God used them to bring forth the Messiah, the Savior of mankind. God had a plan for each of these women. God used them, and how others felt about them, or the opinions others had of them did not change God's mind about using them.

The color you chose for today red can represent so many things: power, danger, anger, and rage, women from the red-light district, but most importantly red represents the blood of Jesus.

The blood that Jesus shed for our redemption cleanses us from past sins.

God gives each of us an opportunity to repent and be forgiven, for past sins, and all who do so are covered by the blood of Jesus.

When a person is covered by the blood of Jesus, it means the price was paid for their freedom from sin. It means that Jesus, God's son paid the price by the shedding of his precious blood. Jesus paid the debt that we owed.

It does not matter how deeply stained your life may have been, God can clean you up and make you become as lamb's wool; white.

In our reference scripture we find two words crimson and scarlet. Crimson was like the stain of blood. Scarlet is defined as a color at the end of the color spectrum, resembling the color of blood, cherries, tomatoes, or rubies. Both colors crimson and scarlet cannot be easily washed out because they are color fast. They standout, they draw a person's attention to them.

These two colors also represent the life that is stained with sin.

When a person sins, their sins are ever before God. **Psalms 51:3** reads *For I know my transgressions, and my sin is always before me;* not only are the sinner aware of their sins, but God is also. That is the point Isaiah 1:18 makes, nothing can make a stained life clean again, except the blood of God's son, Jesus, Christ our Savior.

God promises that if a person repents of their sin, the guilt of the past, deep-dyed as it might be, can be washed away, and leave the sinful person with a restored purity, and it is done by the blood of Jesus.

If a person's soul has been stained, bleaching that soul is the work of God. He alone can *transform* them that they should be "white as snow."

So, it does not matter what your red use to represent or what you use to do or may have done, God is a God of a second chance. He is the one who can clean you up and use you for His purpose. And He can do this even for a woman from the red-light district.

Both Crimson and Scarlet are stand-out colors, glaring, and it is the color that most prostitutes or harlots or ladies of the night put in the window or in the doorway of their homes to signal to potential clients letting them know they are available.

Women from the red-light district lives have an indelible mark placed on them by others and to them they are and never will be any good. But God can bring about a change in the vilest person's life. Though your sins be like scarlet God can wash them white as snow.

It is the precious blood that Jesus shed on Calvary that cleanses us from our sins. John puts it this way in **1ˢᵗ John 1:7** *"the blood of Jesus cleanses us from all sin."* If we have accepted Jesus into our hearts we are "covered by the blood", and our past no matter how wretched it might have been is under the blood.

Never forget that it was because God chose to use women from the red-light district that we are given salvation. You see, those women paved the way for the birth of Jesus Christ our Savior. The plans God had for the women in Jesus' bloodline led to His ultimate plan of Salvation.

How do each of the five women mentioned earlier fit into the birth of Jesus, the Christ? I'm so glad you asked.

Tamar the woman who played the harlot with Judah had twins Pharez and Zerah. Pharez begat Hezron, Hezron begat Ram, Ram begat Amminadab and Amminadab begat Nahshon, and Nashon begat Salmon.

Salmon married **Rehab** the once prostitute from Jericho, and they had a son named Boaz.

Boaz married **Ruth** the women who acted like a prostitute down at the threshing floor and they had a son named Obed. Obed had a son named Jesse and Jesse had a son named David who became king.

King David had a son by **Bathsheba**, the wife of Uriah's who played the harlot with David and that son's name was Solomon. And after some more begetting here comes the **Virgin Mary,** who gave birth to our Lord and Savior Jesus Christ.

You don't have to be perfect for God to use you. For if God can use a woman from the red-light district, he can certainly use you, and you, and anyone who submits their life to him.

May your red represent that you have been washed in the blood of Jesus, Christ the "Lamb of God" and he has washed the stain that sin left on you away. If that is the case, you too are in the bloodline of Jesus because you have been adopted into the family of God.

If you have been redeemed by the lamb of God, your past no longer holds you in bondage to sin; you were in His plan of Salvation and never forget that the plan was fulfilled when five women with questionable reputations followed the plans that God had for their lives.

God chose to use them rather than throw them away.

Perhaps you too have made mistake, you've sin and feel as if you do not have a purpose and your life has no meaning. This message is for you. God does have a plan for your life; surrender to Him and He will make His perfect will known to you.

God stands really to forgive you, redeem you, and use you for His glory.

Let your red represent that you have surrendered your life to God, and you are now covered by the blood of His son Jesus. Christ, our Savior.

God loves us. **John 3:16,17 NIV** reiterates loud and clear, *For God so loved the world that he gave his one and only Son, that whoever believes in him shall not perish but have eternal life. For God did not send his Son into the world to condemn the world, but to save the world through him.* [18] *Whoever believes in him is not condemned...*

My question to you is do you believe?

I cannot speak for you, but I believe. Do you want to know what I believe; I'll tell you anyway.

The Apostle Creed

I believe in God, the Father Almighty, Maker of heaven and earth; and in Jesus Christ, His only Son our Lord who was conceived by the Holy Spirit, born of the virgin Mary, suffered under Pontius Pilate, was crucified, dead and buried. The third day He arose from the dead; He ascended into heaven and sitteth at the right hand of God, the Father Almighty; from then He shall come to judge the quick and the dead. I believe in the Holy Spirit, the holy catholic church, the communion of saints, the forgiveness of sins, the resurrection of the body and the life everlasting. Amen

Chapter 39

The Invitation

No message or sermon is complete without extending an invitation for anyone who has not accepted Jesus, Christ as their personal savior to do so.

Most preachers will say something like this "the doors of the church are open"; but what does that mean?

In most Christian churches this is an altar call where those who wish to make a new spiritual commitment to Jesus Christ are invited to come forward and do so publicly.

If you are reading this book, you may or may not be in a church setting, but God is everywhere and if you have read something in this book that has touched your heart and now you are made aware of your need to accept Jesus, Christ into your life you can right where you are.

No, you do not have to be in a church, but right where you are, all you must do is acknowledge that you are a sinner, ask Jesus Christ to forgive you of your sins, confess that you want Jesus to come into your life and believe that he has heard your prayer, and he will do just that.

It is not a complicated process, but it does hinge on your faith.

You are worth more than what you are feeling right now, you are worth more than the bad opinions some people may have about you or even the bad things some have said about you. You are God's creation and He created you for a purpose.

Recorded in **Psalm 139:14** are these words *"You are fearfully and wonderfully made"* NIV. It is God who created us all, and when we have become broken, it is He who can put us back together again.

It is God who made us and when our lives have been stained by past sins, it is He who will wash us and make us clean.

For that reason, God made a way that when the enemy accuses us, God calls unto us and forgives us, cleans us up and restores us.

If you have been broken by the words, actions, and deeds of others toward you, Let God put you back together again.

You are in God's Plan of Salvation.

God's Plan of Salvation

God said that all who sin will die, both physically and spiritually. This is the fate of all mankind.

But God, in His grace and mercy, provided a way out of this dilemma, by offering each person the right to receive eternal life. He did this by the shedding of the blood of His Son Jesus, the Christ on the cross. God said that *"without the shedding of blood, there is no forgiveness"* **(Hebrews 9:22),** but through the shedding of blood, redemption is provided.

The Law of Moses in **(Exodus 20:2-27)** provided a way for the people to be considered "without sin" or "right" in God's eyes by the offering of animals that were sacrificed for the sins that the people had committed. These sacrifices did not last, and they only were a foreshadowing of Jesus, the one who was without any sin, and sacrificed his life on the cross for mankind. **(Hebrews 10:10).**

Jesus came and died to become the ultimate and final sacrifice, for the sins of mankind. Jesus was that prefect lamb of God who did not have a blemish.

It is through Jesus Christ, the Messiah, that all who believe in God and in His son receives eternal life. This is given to all believers by faith. This promise is extended to all who believe. **(Galatians 3:22)**

The Plan of Salvation is offered to all who have "faith" and who "believe". What we believe is this: Jesus Christ shed his precious blood on an old, rugged cross on a hill called Calvary. After he suffered bled and died, was laid in a tomb, on the third day he got up with all power in his hands, just like he had said he would do, and he is alive for evermore.

Salvation is a gift of God, and it was His plan to save His creation from eternal damnation.

You are in God's Plan of Salvation.

Romans 10:9-10 KJV That *if thou shalt confess with thy mouth the Lord Jesus, and shalt believe in thine heart that God hath raised him from the dead, thou shalt be saved. For with the heart man believeth unto righteousness; and with the mouth confession is made unto salvation.*

Women From the Red-Light District

Who Were in God's Plans of Salvation

Work Cited

Scripture quotations marked NIV are taken from the Holy Bible, New International Version, NIV copyright © 1973, 1978, 1984, 2011 by Biblica, Inc. "Used by permission of Zondervan. All rights reserved worldwide web. wwwzondervan.com

Scripture taken from The Expanded Bible. Copyright ©2011 by Thomas Nelson. Used by permission. All rights reserved

Scriptures marked KJV are taken from the Holy Bible, King James Version

Scriptures marked NLT are taken from the New Living Translation. Tyndale House Publishers, Wheaton, III: Tyndale House Publishers, 2004

Anthony Brown & group therAPy - Worth Lyrics | AZLyrics. com https://www.azlyrics.com/lyrics/anthonybrown/worth.html Feb. 26, 2017

Apostle Creed MLA (7th ed.) Felix, Richard. The Apostles' Creed. Pilot Grove, Mo: Our Faith Press, 1935

More Books by the Author

Death can be compared to a raging storm, for its effects can be just as devastating. While in a storm, you don't know what the outcome will be-you just have to wait it out. The same thing applies to the storms of life and death, the outcome of each ultimately are in God's hands.

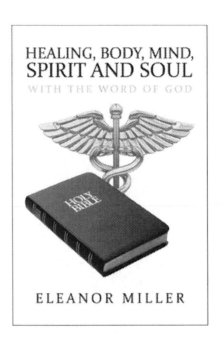

HEALING, BODY, MIND,
SPIRIT AND SOUL
WITH THE WORD OF GOD

ELEANOR MILLER

This book Healing for the Body, Mind, Spirit, and Soul is a compilation of some of the sermons the author has preached over the years. The sermons have brought comfort to many, given strength to others, and provided a way of release to many who have been perplexed by some of life's problems.

COVERED
BY THE LEAVES

WRITTEN BY
REV. ELEANOR D. MILLER

The tree's spell bounding aura caused me to wonder what it would say if it could talk... The year had sped by, and it was now late November, winter would soon be upon us and surely by now the leaves had all fallen to the ground or been divested away by the wind. Yet as I approached the spot where the tree stood, my eyes were still drawn in its direction. Slowly inching my way within an arm's length to the tee, I found myself standing underneath the largest bough and then I waw it, a rope, with a noose dangling at the end. I no longer wondered about what stories this old tree could tell because without saying a word it had already told me more than I really wanted to know. The tree served only to fan the flames of my employment discontentment.

Some years ago, I had the opportunity to speak at a women's prayer breakfast in my hometown. The theme for that prayer breakfast was "Christian Women, showing Compassion and Making a Difference". In contemplating what I would use for a subject, God gave me the message "Let Your Light Shine". The message came from Matthew chapter 5 verses 1-15, but the main thought came from verse 14 where Jesus told his disciples "You are the light of the world". This book is a direct result of the thoughts that God gave me. That message was not only for those gathered for the prayer breakfast, but it was for me also. I had found my purpose, which was and still is to be alight, one that shines forth for Jesus Christ.

Printed in the United States
by Baker & Taylor Publisher Services